STANDUP
COMEDIANS ON TELEVISION

HARRY N. ABRAMS, INC., PUBLISHERS

THE MUSEUM OF TELEVISION & RADIO

Stand-Up Comedians on Television is published in
conjunction with an exhibition of the same title at
The Museum of Television & Radio, New York and
California, March 18–September 29, 1996

The exhibition is made possible by General Motors

For The Museum of Television & Radio:

DIRECTOR OF PUBLICATIONS: *Ellen O'Neill*
CURATOR: *David Bushman*
PHOTOGRAPH EDITOR: *Roberta Panjwani*
ART DIRECTOR: *Lou Dorfsman*

The Museum of Television & Radio is located at
25 West 52 Street, New York, NY 10019–6101 and at
465 North Beverly Drive, Beverly Hills, CA 90210–4654

For Harry N. Abrams, Inc.:

EDITOR: *Robert Morton*
DESIGNER: *Ellen Nygaard Ford*

Library of Congress Cataloging-in-Publication Data

Stand-up comedians on television / essay by Larry Gelbart; interview
    by George Plimpton; curatorial essay by David Bushman.
    p.   cm.
    Includes index.
    ISBN 0–8109–4467–7 (Abrams: cloth) / ISBN 0–8109–2653–9 (Mus. pbk.)
    1. Television comedies—United States. Stand-up comedy—United States.
I. Museum of Television & Radio (New York, N.Y.)
PN1992.8. C66S72 1996
791.45'617—dc20   95–37222

Copyright © 1996 The Museum of Television & Radio
Published in 1996 by Harry N. Abrams, Incorporated, New York
A Times Mirror Company
All rights reserved. No part of the contents of this book may be reproduced
without the written permission of the publisher
Printed and bound in Japan

Previous pages: The Jackie Gleason Show
Opposite: Milton Berle

General Motors's commitment to sharing the "American Experience" is perhaps no better served than by the folkloric storytelling of the American comic. Our comedy defines us as people of a nation. Our humor—the things we find funny, the things we make fun of—is profoundly shaped by our collective experience.

Through all of our diversity, comedy, as an uninhibited mode of expression, helps us achieve a better understanding of ourselves and each other. The stand-up comic, from Milton Berle to Bill Cosby to Jerry Seinfeld, takes a more honest look at ourselves than few others dare.

This book honors those who, through the power of television, have come into our homes and brought families, cultures, and generations together in the spirit of laughter.

The men and women of General Motors recognize the importance and value of comedy as a true reflection of the "American Experience," and their commitment to sharing it with the public is celebrated in The Museum of Television & Radio's salute to American stand-up comedians.

GM General Motors

Foreword

The Museum of Television & Radio is very pleased and excited to bring to life this book celebrating the wit and artistry of the stand-up comedian. The Museum is dedicated to the collection and preservation of our extraordinary heritage of television and radio programs, and most importantly, to making the collection easily accessible to the general public. With a collection of more than 75,000 radio and television programs and advertisements—ranging from drama, comedy, sports, and the performing arts to news, documentaries, and children's programming—students and fans, scholars and journalists, the creative community and aspiring artists can all learn from the masters of the past and build upon their work.

Since opening its doors to the public in 1976, the Museum has created numerous exhibitions. By focusing on the diverse artists whose radio and television legacy are a part of the collection—from maestro Arturo Toscanini, director Herb Brodkin, and writers Levinson and Link to the choreographer Balanchine and comedians Ball, Gleason, Burnett, and Hope—the Museum can give the public an understanding of the historical, social, and artistic significance of the programming.

Our focus here turns to the modern-day stand-up comedian. Funny men and women have been a part of the American entertainment landscape in different guises since the very beginnings of the nation. Following a path from the eighteenth-

century lecture circuit to vaudeville and then radio, the lone wit found a permanent place on television in variety shows, talk shows, game shows, and the genre that has often dominated the medium—situation comedies. The Museum's look at the work of television's comedians in this book should bring all of us insight into the ways in which laughter has dealt with the nation's collective unconscious.

Our television curator David Bushman had the most arduous task of selecting which shows, routines, or appearances to screen in the exhibition from the wealth of material by Benny and Burns and Berle, Reiser and Allen and DeGeneres. As conceived by our director of publications Ellen O'Neill, the book adds another dimension to the exhibition by bringing together many different voices—critics, novelists, comedy writers—to look at and muse upon a half-century of comedians loosely grouped by the content of their humor: Working-Class Stiffs, Modern Angst, Men vs. Women, and so on.

For this endeavor, we would like to acknowledge the support of General Motors, whose sponsorship has made the exhibition and this book possible. GM's participation with the Museum on this project underscores the continued commitment to quality television it has demonstrated throughout the years.

In the end, it is the material itself that the Museum collects, preserves, and presents to the general public that deserves attention. The talent, artistry, and hard work of the individual stand-up comedians have earned our applause, and now our praise. In the words of one of the greatest, ". . . and away we go!"

Robert M. Batscha
President
The Museum of Television & Radio

Seinfeld

Opposite:
Woody Allen on *The Tonight Show Starring Johnny Carson*

Roseanne

Contents

Send Out the Clowns

by Larry Gelbart

Take my life. Please. There was a time when, if I wanted to catch the work of a stand-up comic, or a monologuist as they were called then, I would have to go through the trouble and expense of traveling to a nightclub, a vaudeville house, or a house of burlesque. I would have to sit through endless hours of acrobats and ecdysiasts, of hearing G chords and ogling G-strings, until the band finally hit "Fine and Dandy," and the guy with the padded shoulders and the porkpie hat came on to stand in the spotlight and tell the audience all about the funny thing that happened to him on his way to the theater that night.

(To digress for a moment—and just to establish the convention—the best switch I ever heard on that stock opening was delivered by a wanted-to-be comic named Arthur Loewe, Jr., whose opening line at a flood benefit was, "Good evening, ladies and gentlemen. A funny thing happened to the theater on its way to me tonight.")

As it would affect and reshape so much of modern life, from religion to politics, from sports to the justice system, to the act of re-creating life itself, broadcasting also changed the stand-up world. No longer did the members of an audience have to assemble somewhere outside their homes to be in the presence of the comics. Broadcasting delivered the comics directly to the audience. Broadcasting sent out the clowns. First, via radio, where we found them in our ears; then, later, on television, where we find them in our faces. If broadcasting delivered the comedians, the comedians more than delivered for broadcasting. Were it remotely possible to quantify such a thing, the profits, the staggering zillions, that the providers of laughter have generated for network and cable companies, for syndicators and affiliates, would offer stunning evidence of the power of the punch line to affect the bottom line.

Comics—that gifted, exclusive society of professional fools—have proven themselves to be the most durable commodity on the box. Western stars have come and gone thataway. The most popular of prime-time doctors eventually find their viewers refusing their house calls. But the comic is a constant. Clearly, we need laughter more than we need a sheriff, a smile far more than surgery. With apologies to my friend, Stephen Sondheim, comedy tonight is not what it's about. Comedy is forever.

With good reason. The stand-up comedian bestows upon the viewer a unique and precious gift. The stand-up elevates the viewer to royalty. As kings and queens, we watch in our robes or in our underwear as these supplicants do their shtick, each a petitioner for our approval, each our very own, personal court jester, wanting only to win our favor, in the hope that they may someday be granted a sitcom of their own, so that they, too, can achieve their own stardom. And we, who will spend billions to attend lavish, gargantuan movies with eye-boggling special effects, spend much more time simply watching an appearance, on a one-on-one basis, by a single person, whose only special effects are language and a point of view. (Comic talents such as Robin Williams and Richard Pryor, can, however, in themselves seem as though they are a cast of thousands.) Is it an exaggeration to say that we pay more undivided attention to a stand-up than we do to other members of our household? We don't quarrel with the stand-ups. We don't counter one of their jokes with one of our own. We are their quiet, respectful partners. Monologuists they may be, but our thoughtful participation turns their solo routines into a dialogue.

It seems the most inevitable and fortuitous of marriages: television and the practitioners of stand-up comedy. Basically, television has always been about people watching (with an occasional break to watch animals doing to each other what respectable television won't let us see people do to each other). The TV monitor forms the perfect frame for the human face; in close-up, the scale is life size. During a stand-up's performance, that is not a picture of a person talking to us—that is a real person, a real person performing on a stage in New York City to an audience whose last row is sitting in California. Or the other way around, or in any other possible direction, for the medium has turned the whole country into one vast comedy club. Having a performer literally at our fingertips makes for an intimacy that allows our comics to deal with the one subject in the world that we can never get enough of. That subject, of course, is us: what we look like, how we grew up, how we didn't, how we relate, how we don't.

Comics are journalists; they are the correspondents of our common experiences, the cruise directors of the same boat we're all in together. They goad us with truths we would often rather ignore or deny. They update us on the human and all-too-often inhuman condition. The stand-up spot is a soapbox, a pulpit, or a confessional. The best comedians hold up a mirror to themselves, wherein we see our own captured reflection. They address our fears, our dreams; they examine our secret bits and parts—the ones under our clothes, the ones under our hats. Using comedy as anesthesia allows them to deal with the dark, underbelly laughs we employ as a defense against life's pains, its embarrassments, and its frustrations.

In the seventies and the eighties, as the contracts with life of the legendary comedy stars started running out, a premature wake began for the death of comedy itself. Without the age-old training grounds for comedians—the stage shows, the Catskills, the tank towns—where was anyone ever going to get the experience and the confidence eventually to get a shot at TV? Where was all the new talent going to come from? The answer, it turns out, was that they were going to come from everywhere. From out of the woodwork, from colleges, from amateur improv groups, from TV itself. The *Tonight Show* in its many incarnations and *Saturday Night Live*, among others, act as beginner slopes for novice stand-ups, the diamonds in the rough, as well as the hopelessly zircon, whose careers often turn out to be far shorter than the limos that pick them up for their trip to the studio.

The truth is that comedians, in any age and in any technological environment, come from only one place. They come from themselves. What they put on for our benefit are the external performances of the ones that play constantly inside their heads. Their compulsion is our gain. The seemingly frivolous nature of their craft belies their incredible bravery. They try, as comic tadpoles, facing what seem like faceless crowds that can turn hostile on a bon mot's notice, armed only with their wits. However many might be deterred, they never stop filling up the four corners of our screens. We may have a choice about whether or not they have chosen the right career for themselves, but they do not. They have to do what they are doing. And they will do it if tens of millions are watching, or, if after counting the house, they find that the audience, plus them, equals two. On and on, they come. On and on, the band plays their intros, and they enter through the curtain, as they did even before anyone even thought about building the road for the first chicken to cross. Whether they stand before us in a suit or a dress, in a tux or in drag, they are naked. They are working without a net, they are flying solo. Of course, we are not talking about life and death here. A stand-up comedian is not a matador. When a matador enters the ring, he is assisted in his performance against the bull by two picadors, atop two horses, and three banderilleros. Six men and two animals to subdue and master one beast. The comic faces the beast alone. Unaided, often blinded by the very spotlight he or she is so desperate to bask in, the comic must dominate and control the adversary with no help from anyone at all, with the possible exception of an agent praying in the wings.

Rewind: maybe we are talking about life and death here. When stand-ups talk about having had a good night, they talk about how they killed the audience, how they slayed them, how they really put them away. Or about how they, the comics, failed; how they really died last night. Vast amounts of resentment mingle with the comedian's love for and dependence upon the audience. The audience is, after all, the last great obstacle that must be overcome if the stand-up's debut is to be a success on Johnny or David or Jay. This total reliance upon total strangers who have tuned in to catch your act, some of whom might possibly be just a little too high, while others of them might possibly be just a little too low, to appreciate the routine that you have labored so long and so hard to perfect makes for an understandable and altogether maddening ambivalence.

Today's practitioners of comedy differ greatly from those we've laughed at in the past. One branch of the current crop of stand-ups, those influenced by the new three "R's"—rock, raunch, and race—make it clear that there are no longer any bounds, there are no barriers, and very often, little or no taste at all. They act as so many lepidopterists, pricking our shared pomposities and pretensions and pinning us to the wall, by whatever means necessary, with fair language or foul. And who are we to yell "Foul," we who are arrogant enough to believe that there is life on no other planet, while guaranteeing through our ignorance and indifference that before too long there may not be any on this one either. If you would judge the moral climate of our society, listen to our behavior as it is blown back into our faces with such relentless and accurate comic force.

George Plimpton on Stand-Up Comedy:
A Paris Review *Inquiry*

Q: I understand that in your career as a participatory journalist you once tried a stint as a stand-up comic.

A: That is true. Years ago. It was a very brief engagement (indeed only one night) at Caesar's Palace in Las Vegas—in theory the climax of a documentary special for ABC on the art of comedy. The special, from 1971, was entitled *Plimpton! Did You Hear the One About . . .?* I had the privilege of being coached for the Big Night by a remarkable cast of comedians, all of whom had careers as stand-up comics— Buddy Hackett, Bob Hope, Woody Allen, Phyllis Diller, Steve Allen, Jonathan Winters, among them. Not only that, but I had a routine written for me by the star writers of one of the most successful television shows ever—a rube-dominated show called *Laugh-In.*

Q: Was the stint successful?

A: It could hardly be classified as a "wow." Agents did not crowd backstage into my dressing room afterward to sign me up for the Catskills. Looking back, there were a number of problems. The routine prepared for me, full of Howard Hughes and John Wayne jokes, didn't seem very appropriate. In fact, I went to the two writers and complained that they had not captured my style. They said to me as follows: "Plimpton, if we could capture your style, we'd put it in a cage and club it to death." Actually, that was a much funnier remark than anything they'd given me to say on the stage of Caesar's Palace.

Q: What sort of advice did you get?

A: Well, the weirdest piece of advice came from Jonathan Winters. He suggested that for my entrance I should pull back the curtain just a bit, sticking my head out like a man peeking out from behind a shower curtain, and in a somewhat simpering voice say, "Hi!"

Q: Did you do that?

A: Absolutely not.

Q: What was your problem out there?

A: I speak rather slowly with the accents my parents endowed me with—a sort of Boston Brahmin. My old friend, the actor Martin Gabel, Brooklyn-born, when asked about his rather cultivated accent would reply, "Affected, my dear sir, affected." Mine might be considered as such, but isn't. Whatever, it isn't at all suitable for stand-up comedy. It's a bit as if William F. Buckley had suddenly turned up on the borscht circuit. Steve Allen, who was one of my coaches, kept telling me I sounded too much like Cordell Hull, who was one of the more solemn statesmen of the time. He kept saying: "Try to sound less like Cordell Hull." Moreover, I wore a dinner jacket, black bow tie, black glistening pumps, the props of elegance—hardly what one sees walk out onto the stage of the comedy clubs these days.

Q: Did they prepare you for dealing with hecklers?

A: I vaguely recall that I was told that if a waiter dropped a plate I was supposed to call out, "Pick up your teeth!" Actually, in such an instance I probably would have cried out, "My God, the shoe is poisoned."

A: Why that?

Q: It's one of the most famous ad-libs—the only one I know. It was Edwin Booth's. In a duel scene onstage he was supposed to fall mortally wounded by a gunshot, but his opponent couldn't get his pistol to fire. *Click, click, click.* Eventually, in his frustration, he went up and kicked Booth in the behind . . . at which point Booth delivered the ad-lib, "My God, the shoe is poisoned," and fell to the floor. Terrific stuff!

Q: Not a very appropriate ad-lib if someone's plate falls to the floor.

A: Agreed.

Q: How would you redefine your act if you had to perform today?

A: In these times I would be completely worthless. The reason would be that I am unable either to tell dirty jokes or to talk dirty, which sadly is a necessity today. I grew up in a family in which the most modest of scatological words and phrases were never uttered. My mother's favorite epithet was, "Ye Gods!" If my father ran the family car into a truck loaded with crates of chickens, that is what she would cry out, "Ye Gods!" My father's designated term for the truck driver, however foul the language he was being belted with as the two faced each other out on the street, was invariably "sonny," as in, "Sonny, you should have your driver's license removed." I suppose if I went off somewhere and learned to swear like the aforementioned truck driver—storming at the waves of the Long Island Sound like a modern day Demosthenes—it might prepare me for the next step, the move to the brick wall, where I would deliver a rather nervous dissertation, say, about multiple orgasms.

Q: A brick wall?

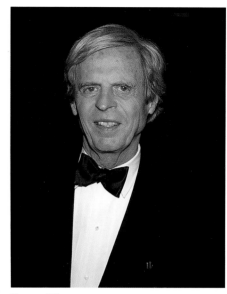

George Plimpton, 1994

A: That's what they are these days—brick-wall comedians. Inevitably, to deliver their routines, they're standing before a brick wall—as if somehow that prop is as necessary to their performance as baggy pants and a flat hat were to the second-banana comedians of the heyday of vaudeville. So is what the comics wear in the nineties—invariably jeans, often worn to a frazzle, an unbuttoned shirt, with a black T-shirt underneath, and a baseball cap, usually worn backwards. I can't imagine any of them walking out in front of the brick wall wearing a tuxedo.

Q: Why are the routines these days as vulgar as they are?

A: The audiences have a lot to do with it . . . younger people by far. They have discretionary funds to spend and, alas, not much discretion of taste. The makeup of audiences not so long ago was entirely different—older, more sophisticated—and vulgarity would have little appeal. Actually, vulgarity is seeping into the routines of established older stand-up comics. I heard Mike Nichols recall a Joan Rivers joke he'd heard her tell in England: "The day I have multiple orgasms is the day Stevie Wonder hits a hole in one." That seems to me tasteless on *two* counts, which is difficult in a single sentence.

Q: How essential is this sort of approach?

A: Neil Simon once said that to say the F-word once in a play is far more shocking than to say it fifty times. He says, "I love language, and I'd rather find other ways to use it than take the easy way out." That is obviously something the new comics do not subscribe to. As a friend of mine once put it, "When it's third and long yardage, they go to dope and sex." But one must remember that the stock-in-trade of the stand-up comic is traditionally material that is subversive. If it isn't, the routine tends to be somewhat bland. This kind of venomous approach goes back a long way. The historians tell us about L'Angley, the royal fool during the reign of Louis XIV, who from his station at table behind the king so terrified members of the court that he was finally banished for his impertinence. A British fool (he bore a rather unlikely name for a clown, Archibald Armstrong), who served in the reigns of James I and Charles I, was eventually dismissed for a jest involving an Archbishop Laud. In the presence of the archbishop he gave the following grace: "Great praise be to God and little Laud praise to the devil!"—a Latin pun on his name that infuriated the archbishop.

Q: That doesn't sound especially lewd or salacious.

A: A very sensitive archbishop, I agree. But I suspect a royal court was very much on edge if the jesters were truly on their feed. Traditionally a jester was an outsider looking in; in the early days he was very often a dwarf, or disfigured in some way, or at the very least outlandishly dressed in order to emphasize this distance. But it also meant he could get away with savage quips about his betters. In the modern era of the stand-up comics, they, too, have been outsiders looking in—inevitably members of a minority, often persecuted—Jews, Irish, blacks, Hispanics.

Q: So you'd recommend being a minority before testing the stand-up comic waters?

A: You should know before testing the waters that a directory referred to as the *1995 Comedy USA* lists 5,000 comics. Though laughter is pretty much a universal commodity, that's probably far too many. I am truly hard-pressed to name more than ten or fifteen. The odds against becoming a successful stand-up comic are overwhelming. Then, there's one more thing to consider.

Q: What's that?

A: One day one is sure to perform before an audience of Alexander Popes.

Q: Why Alexander Pope?

A: He boasted that he had never laughed in his life.

THE STAND-UP COMEDIAN

Jack Benny

Bill Cosby

ON TELEVISION

by David Bushman

Roseanne

Writing forty years ago, in the era of Berle, Benny, Gleason, and Caesar, media critic Gilbert Seldes called comedy the "axis on which broadcasting revolves." Today, in the age of Seinfeld, Allen, Letterman, and Roseanne, who would argue?

Tellingly, all of these contemporary performers have at least one thing in common: a background in stand-up comedy. And all four of the earlier comedians, while not known as stand-ups in their time, came to television with backgrounds in comedy that in some way foreshadowed stand-up as we know it today.

This idiosyncratic breed of funny men and women has played a vital role in the evolution of television from the start—television's first superstar, Milton Berle, had performed stand-up monologues for more than twenty years before he hosted his first installment of *The Texaco Star Theater*.

For five decades, television has crowned stand-up comedy's kings and queens, carrying their wit, wisdom, and lunacy to audiences far and wide. And in those huge television audiences have been young men and women who, seduced by the excitement of watching comedians perform on the likes of *The Ed Sullivan Show, The Tonight Show, The Hollywood Palace,* and *The Kraft Music Hall,* have been inspired to pursue stand-up careers of their own, no matter how daunting the odds or how painful the consequences.

And they can be painful. "Life isn't easy, folks," Rodney Dangerfield tells his audiences, and for once he isn't joking. Life for stand-up comedians *isn't* easy. Ask Wally Cox, who once bombed so badly at the Dunes in Las Vegas that the hotel had him wheeled out on a stretcher so it could announce that his engagement was being canceled due to illness. "Laughter," Robin Williams once said, invoking the spirit of Lenny Bruce, "is reinforcing; it's wonderful when people laugh. And when they don't laugh, it's more painful

Jackie Gleason

Tim Allen

Jerry Seinfeld

Sid Caesar

David Letterman

than fiberglass underwear." (For a civilian's experience of performing stand-up, see George Plimpton, page 14.)

While the term "stand-up comedian" was not widely used until the sixties, the American tradition of oral comedy is long and rich, at least as old as the nineteenth-century Yankee yarn-spinners and tall-tale-tellers of the Missouri Valley like Davy Crockett. Abraham Lincoln was an inveterate joke teller who mastered the art of storytelling at a country store and could not resist a witty epigram. Mark Twain moonlighted as a platform lecturer, ferociously satirizing fanaticism, hypocrisy, injustice, and sentimentality.

The Berles, Bennys, Seinfelds, and Lettermans of the television world are the descendants of these and other pioneers of American oral comedy. This book is an exploration of how comedians of the television age have continued the American comedy tradition and brought their own perspectives to bear on the vagaries of modern times. Further, it is a celebration of the indefatigable American comedic spirit, which has endured—even flourished—through wars, depressions, oppression, the sexual revolution, and the threat of nuclear annihilation. Comedy, particularly stand-up comedy, mirrors the American experience; the moods and preoccupations of the country are reflected in the faces and contents and voices of the people who perform it. And for the past fifty years, television has been there to capture, preserve, and even help create it.

WHO IS A STAND-UP?

Both the Oxford English Dictionary and Webster's Ninth New Collegiate trace the origin of the term "stand-up comedian" to 1966 and essentially define the stand-up comic as someone whose act is performing a succession of jokes or otherwise humorous comments while standing alone before an audience. Using this definition, comedians like Jerry Seinfeld, Bill Cosby, and Richard Pryor are instantly recognizable as stand-ups. But in many cases, the distinction is

Mark Twain

not so clear. For example, comedians like Bob Newhart, Don Adams, and Shelley Berman (called nightclub comedians rather than stand-up comics when they broke into the business in the late fifties and early sixties) specialized in monologues structured more like one-person sketches than classic stand-up routines. Similarly, comedy teams like the Smothers Brothers, Rowan and Martin, and Nichols and May are not stand-ups in the strictest sense, because in each case the members of the team address each other onstage more than they do the audience. But comedians from both these groups are strikingly similar to pure stand-ups in an essential way: all perform humorous material before live audiences largely unsupported by elaborate props, scenery, dramatic narrative, or supporting casts. There is a rawness and fearlessness to their work that elevates them to heroic stature, particularly in an age in which technology threatens to overwhelm—if not annihilate—the individual.

Further, comedians like Jack Benny, Milton Berle, Fred Allen, Jackie Gleason, and Sid Caesar were working in vaudeville, nightclubs, and/or vacation resorts in upstate New York decades before the term "stand-up comedy" even existed, but were performing a type of comedy that involved essential elements of pure stand-up and anticipated stand-

up as we know it today. The pages that follow will address the work of these and other pre-sixties comedians as well.

Lastly, because the subject of this book is stand-up comedians on television—rather than stand-up comedy—we will explore sitcoms and sketch comedy that, while not stand-up routines themselves, are performed by stand-up-style comedians and are built upon the sensibilities of their stand-up persona or acts. A case in point: *The Cosby Show,* in which both the subject matter—the day-to-day life of a loving upper-middle-class African-American family in Brooklyn—and Cosby's character were heavily influenced by the comedian's stand-up act, and vice versa.

HISTORICAL STAND-UP

The roots of American stand-up comedy go back to the development of mass entertainment in the mid-nineteenth century. Between 1830 and 1860 America's population doubled, big cities began sprouting up, and the railroad revolutionized transportation, creating new urban audiences—largely male, immigrant, and illiterate—who demanded entertainment that was cheap and simple. It was in this environment that American mass entertainment first flourished—in the form of minstrelsy, a coarse, frenetic breed of variety show in which white performers appeared in blackface and spoke in exaggerated black dialects. And it is in minstrelsy that we see two of the earliest ancestors of the stand-up comedian: the end men and the stump speaker.

As Mel Watkins recounts in his seminal book on African-American humor, *On the Real Side,* the first of the minstrel show's three acts was dominated by a pair of flamboyant comedians called end men; they dressed outrageously, mugged shamelessly, and fired off simplistic puns, quips, and riddles of the sort that would one day become a staple of burlesque houses and American adolescent humor (like, "Why did the chicken cross the road?"). Act two was highlighted by the stump speaker, whose monologues

ranged from pure nonsense to lampoons of social or philo-
sophical issues.

The late nineteenth century saw another progenitor of
the stand-up comedian, the comic lecturer. The best known
of the bunch, most of whom had begun as newspaper
columnists with bizarre pen names that they took to the
platform lecture, included Mark Twain, Artemus Ward, and
Petroleum Vesuvius Nasby. Typically their humor derived
from malapropisms, atrocious grammar, exaggeration, and
incongruity, but their intentions varied. Ward loved puns
and plays on words; Nasby was more biting (his favorite targets were states' rights and white supremacy); Twain started
out as a pure humorist, but evolved into a bitter satirist.

In the last decade of the 1800s, vaudeville supplanted
minstrelsy as the dominant form of American entertainment; it would flourish into the twenties—felled at last by
radio and talking pictures—and produce a roster of entertainers who would dominate American comedy for decades.
Most vaudeville-era comedy involved performers addressing
each other onstage, rather than speaking directly to the
audience. Team acts dominated, but monologuists worked
the circuits as well. Will Rogers was the most celebrated, but
Frank Fay, Jack Benny, Fred Allen, Milton Berle, Bob Hope,
and Bert Williams also experimented with direct-address
comedy.

Williams was one of the few African-Americans to cross
over; for all but the most successful and celebrated black
performers, vaudeville remained a closed shop. In 1907, an
alternative network of theaters called the Theater Owners
Booking Association was founded to showcase African-
American talent. The TOBA flourished into the thirties,
when it, too, fell victim to spiraling technology and the
Great Depression. It was supplanted by the Apollo Theatre
in New York as the crown jewel of black variety entertainment onstage. Like the black tent shows and cabarets that
came before and the nightclubs and "chitlin' circuit" theaters
that followed, the TOBA and the Apollo functioned as shadow
circuits in much the same way that the Negro leagues did in

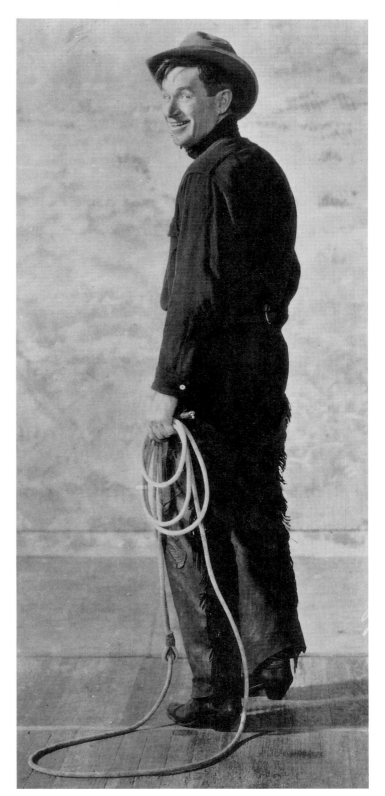

Will Rogers

Jack Benny and Fred Allen in a 1947 radio appearance

Tim Moore *(front)* with Spencer Williams, Jr., and Alvin Childress in *Amos 'n' Andy* (1951–53)

professional baseball, offering many African-Americans their only chance to communicate authentically, without compromising their acts to appease mainstream audiences. Every major black comedian from the first half of this century passed through these circuits, including Pigmeat ("Here come de Judge") Markham, Tim Moore (Kingfish

BOB HOPE

Without question, the stand-up comedian who most influenced me was Frank Fay, vaudeville's top monologuist in the twenties. When I was growing up and had theatrical ambitions, my mother took me to see Frank Fay at Keith's 105th Street in Cleveland. He stood there and talked to the audience as if they were old friends. After Frank had worked for a few minutes, "Mahm" looked at me and said loudly, "He's not half as good as you!" People near looked at us as if we were goofy . . . but Mahm, my biggest morale booster, looked back at them defiantly and stared them down.

from the television version of *The Amos 'n' Andy Show),* Stepin Fetchit, Moms Mabley, Nipsey Russell, Slappy White, and Redd Foxx.

For Jewish comics in the thirties and forties, the borscht belt resorts in the Catskill Mountains of upstate New York similarly served as an alternative outlet for a brand of humor known as shtetl, from the Yiddish word for small town or village. Dubbed humor that, "kept one eye on the exit at all times" by *Esquire* writer Joyce Wadler, borscht belt comedy was for urban, working-class vacationers, and it underscored the differences between Jews and non-Jews rather than pretending they didn't exist. The humor could be rude and crude—Jerry Lewis dumping a bowl of soup on his head or Henny Youngman getting into a food fight. The comics, known as tummlers from the Yiddish word for noise or merrymaking, were responsible for keeping guests laughing not just during performances onstage, but all day everyday and everywhere—poolside, at card games, in dining rooms.

By the end of the forties, as airfare and exotic vacations became more affordable, the golden age of tummler humor had come and gone. But for borscht belt jesters like Sid Caesar, Buddy Hackett, Zero Mostel, Alan King, Mel Brooks, Don Rickles, and Joey Bishop, the resorts had served as an invaluable training ground for bigger—and more lucrative—things, beginning with urban nightclubs. The forties and fifties were boom times for these night spots, led by the fabled Copacabana in New York City. The best known and wealthiest of the clubs favored mainstream comics from the vaudeville and tummler traditions, but in the mid-fifties so-called chi-chi rooms like Mr. Kelly's in Chicago, the hungry i in San Francisco, and the Bitter End in New York emerged as outlets for a new type of comedy practiced by the likes of Lenny Bruce, Dick Gregory, and Mort Sahl. From these venues would emerge much of the comedy that would go on to dominate the American scene for two decades.

In the early and middle sixties, nightclubs continued to breed the best and the brightest of the new comedians, as New York-based performers such as Woody Allen, Bill Cosby, Dick Cavett, Joan Rivers, Lily Tomlin, and Richard Pryor all rose to fame in Greenwich Village. But by the latter part of the decade, many of the old Village haunts had vanished or been turned into rock venues, and as a forum for comedy, the nightclub was giving way to a new phenomenon—the comedy club. Instead of featuring one or two comedians a night in addition to a musical performance, comedy clubs offered all comedy all the time.

By the late sixties, television talent scouts had crowned comedy clubs *the* place to be. Comic Richard Lewis remembers performing night after night at the Improvisation Comedy Club, or the Improv, in midtown Manhattan in the early seventies with Jimmie Walker, Freddie Prinze, and Gabe Kaplan; by 1975, only Lewis was without a sitcom (he eventually got one, *Anything But Love,* but not until 1989). "They'd blow the roof off the Improv," he told Alan King on Comedy Central's *Inside the Comedy Mind.* "I got a taste of what it meant to be pre-known. When they walked on

that stage the people applauded; they didn't have to prove themselves."

Comedy clubs flourished from the mid-seventies to the late eighties before a confluence of factors—including, ironically, competition from television—prompted a shakeout, but their influence remains enormous. Many of today's most influential comedy stars emerged from clubs, including Tim Allen, Jerry Seinfeld, Paul Reiser, Roseanne, Brett Butler, Ellen DeGeneres, Jay Leno, and David Letterman.

STAND-UP ON TELEVISION

In its infancy, decades before these clubs existed, television was driven by such comedy stars as Milton Berle, Jackie Gleason, Jack Benny, and Sid Caesar—first-generation

George Burns with Gleason on *The Jackie Gleason Show* (1952–70)

pioneers who not only established many of the conventions of the medium that still exist today but also legitimized television as an entertainment option. They were the first television performers to serve as role models for generations of comedians to come. As Larry Gelbart points out in his essay (see page 10), television brings comedy to the people. And in living rooms across the country, impressionable young men and women sit and watch the flickering light, dreaming of one day being on the other side of the screen. Garry Shandling was inspired to pursue a career in comedy by Woody Allen's appearances on *Hot Dog,* a Saturday-morning children's program from the early seventies. Keenan Ivory Wayans can recall exactly what he was doing when he decided to become a comedian—watching Richard Pryor on *The Della Reese Show.* Rita Rudner spent hour upon hour at The Museum of Television & Radio (then called The Museum of Broadcasting) viewing Jack Benny, Woody Allen, and Burns and Allen before embarking on her stand-up career.

On the television landscape, stand-up comedians have made their biggest impact via three genres: the comedy/variety show, the situation comedy, and the talk show. (A fourth genre, the game show, has proved sporadically valuable as well.) The comedy/variety show dominated television comedy in the medium's earliest days, but fell out of favor in the early sixties and has since all but disappeared from American television. For stand-up comics in search of prime-time exposure, it was a palpable loss that can still be felt today. Some have been willing and able to make the leap to sitcoms; others turned to prime-time game shows when they were still in vogue. But neither genre offers the opportunities that comedy/variety does for straight stand-up. In the mid-seventies, however, cable networks began featuring stand-up comedy with full-length concerts by single performers or shorter performances by several comedians in a comedy-club setting. Stand-ups regained significant prime-time exposure—but for a much smaller universe of viewers.

Many of television's most successful comedy/variety

Bob Hope and George Carlin join the host (center) of *The Flip Wilson Comedy Special* (1975)

Red Skelton

shows have been emceed by stand-up-style comedians, including Jackie Gleason, Milton Berle, Sid Caesar, Red Skelton, Flip Wilson, the Smothers Brothers, and Rowan and Martin. In addition, stand-up-style comedians have appeared regularly as guests on comedy/variety shows. By virtue of its popularity and endurance, *The Ed Sullivan Show* (originally called *Toast of the Town*), which ran from

The George Burns and Gracie Allen Show (1950–58) with Hal March,
Bea Benaderet, Gracie Allen, and George Burns

Jeffrey Tambor, Rip Torn, and Garry Shandling on *The Larry Sanders Show* (debuted in 1992)

1948 to 1971, was perhaps the most important prime-time showcase for stand-up comedians.

Typically, stand-up comics function in one or both of two ways on these shows: they either perform solo by doing straight stand-up—five-or-so-minute segments from their longer club routines—or appear in comedic sketches along with other performers. For most stand-up comics making the transition to television, sketch comedy is radically different from their regular act; it requires that they perform within the construct of a narrative structure rather than a simple monologue, and it means that they are no longer performing alone. Some comedians, like Red Skelton, Flip Wilson, Richard Pryor, and Lily Tomlin—specialists in character comedy—often merge the two by building sketches around characters created in their stand-up routines.

By the early sixties, the situation comedy, a transplant from radio, had supplanted comedy/variety as the dominant form of comedy on television. Like sketch comedy, the sitcom requires that the stand-up comedian devise a new way to structure his persona and act. Two of the most prominent early examples were *The Jack Benny Program* and *The George Burns and Gracie Allen Show*. Rather than abandon the comedy/variety genre completely, Benny and Burns and Allen incorporated elements of it into their sitcoms. In mind-bending blurs of reality and fiction, Benny and Burns and Allen played characters with the same names and professions as the real-life comedians. The Burns and Allen program was particularly surreal: Burns often stepped out of the situation comedy and addressed the audience directly, breaking the fourth wall. On occasion he even retired to his study and turned on the television to find out what other characters in the sitcom were up to. Variations of this format have continued to appear ever since; more contemporary viewers will recognize Garry Shandling's *It's Garry Shandling's Show* and *The Larry Sanders Show* and Jerry Seinfeld's *Seinfeld* as descendants.

Sitcoms flourished from the mid-fifties through the early eighties, with stand-up-style comedians playing key roles: Wally Cox (*Mr. Peepers*), Don Adams (*Get Smart*), Bob Newhart (*The Bob Newhart Show* and *Newhart*), Redd Foxx (*Sanford and Son*), Jimmie Walker (*Good Times*), Gabe Kaplan (*Welcome Back, Kotter*), Freddie Prinze (*Chico and the Man*), and Andy Kaufman (*Taxi*). Then, in the 1983–84 season, only one sitcom (*Kate & Allie*) cracked the top ten. The following season, however, the genre was revived almost single-handedly by *The Cosby Show*. Hugely popular with critics and viewers alike and hailed as revolutionary for its sophisticated, nonstereotypical portrayal of an upper-middle-class African-American family, the series finished third in its first year and first in each of its next four. Whole episodes revolved around the death of a pet goldfish or the trouble a child was having applying himself in school—material that could have come straight out of Cosby's stand-up act.

The *Cosby Show* ushered in a new era of sitcoms, many of which were fronted by stand-up comics. *Roseanne,* a blue-collar domestic sitcom that embodies the brash, subversive humor of its star, supplanted *Cosby* as the number one show in 1989, its second season. *Seinfeld,* a minimalist sitcom based on the observational humor of stand-up comedian Jerry Seinfeld, arrived two years later and took longer to catch on, but emerged as one of television's most successful series, inspiring a slew of imitative comedies about "nothing." Granted, there have been multiple failures for every successful sitcom that starred a stand-up comic (anyone remember Lenny Clarke's *Lenny,* John Mendoza's *The Second Half,* or Richard Lewis and Don Rickles's *Daddy Dearest*). But what successes! Tim Allen's *Home Improvement,* Paul Reiser's *Mad About You,* Brett Butler's *Grace Under Fire,* Ellen DeGeneres's *Ellen*—huge hits, every one.

The talk show has been a critical venue for stand-up comedians from the earliest days of the genre, beginning with the 1954 premiere of *The Tonight Show* (then called *Tonight*). Original host Steve Allen not only introduced the stand-up monologue to the genre but also opened the show to young, often nonmainstream comedians unable to gain significant prime-time exposure, a tradition continued by

Judy Carne and Don Rickles on *Rowan and Martin's Laugh-In* (1968–73)

Dan Rowan and Dick Martin

Lenny Bruce and Steve Allen

Jack Paar

David Letterman on *The Tonight Show Starring Johnny Carson* (1962–92)

The Tonight Show with Jay Leno (debuted in 1992)

Arsenio Hall

each of his successors: Jack Paar, Johnny Carson, and Jay Leno—the last two having been stand-up comedians themselves.

David Letterman, another former stand-up, has emerged as a starmaker for stand-up comedians in his own right, first on *Late Night with David Letterman* and now on the *Late Show with David Letterman*. Writing before Carson's 1992 retirement from *The Tonight Show,* critic Tom Shales of the *Washington Post* dubbed Carson and Letterman "the Don Vito Corleone and Michael Corleone of modern American comedy. I wouldn't cross them if I were you and I wanted a career being funny."

Merv Griffin, host of numerous talk shows from 1962 to 1986, developed a reputation for booking not just estab-

Totie Fields, Merv Griffin, and Myron Cohen on *The Merv Griffin Show* (CBS, 1969–72)

lished pros but also up-and-comers like Joan Rivers, Lily Tomlin, David Steinberg, George Carlin, and Richard Pryor. Arsenio Hall, also a stand-up comedian, became the first black to host a successful late-night talk show in 1989; *The Arsenio Hall Show* provided a mainstream outlet for authentic black comedy, and featured many African-Americans who generally found television work hard to come by. *The Mike Douglas Show* (1963–82) also gave important national exposure to stand-up comedians.

STAND-UP AS MIRROR

Academics have argued for centuries over the origins and distinctive characteristics of American humor. Yes, there has always been humor in America, but when was the first concerted output of humor that was distinctly American in sensibility? And what is that sensibility?

The consensus claims that American humor began in earnest in the early nineteenth century with the emergence of native or frontier humorists such as Augustus Baldwin Longstreet, Seba Smith, and James Russell Lowell, whose vernacular, anti-intellectual writings celebrated down-home, unlettered common sense and lampooned intellectualism, effeteness, and city ways—all symbols of British propriety. These cracker-barrel philosophers were soon followed by Mark Twain, Artemus Ward, Josh Billings, and the rest of the so-called Phunny Phellows.

These early practitioners of American humor established archetypes that embodied aspects of the American condition that have endured to this day. The rural Yankee manservant Jonathan in Royall Tyler's seminal 1787 play *The Contrast*—a fish out of water on his visit to New York City—is seen again in the Jewish tummlers of the borscht belt and such African-American comedians as Dick Gregory and Richard Pryor. These are all practitioners of humor based on "intense odd-man-out anxiety," as Kurt Andersen dubs it in his afterward to *Laughing Matters: A Celebration*

Judd Hirsch and Andy Kaufman on *Taxi* (1978–83)

Dan Ackroyd and Steve Martin on *Saturday Night Live* (debuted in 1975)

Robin Williams and Jonathan Winters on *Mork & Mindy* (1978–82)

of American Humor. Andy Kaufman's Latka Gravas, Robin Williams's Mork, and Steve Martin's "wild and crazy" Festrunk brother are television-age incarnations of the same condition—natural enough in a country of immigrants and migrants, of dislocated people straddling two worlds, torn between holding on and fitting in. Similarly, the irreverence of wiseguy comedians like Groucho Marx, David Letterman, and Bob Hope is rooted in the anti-British writings of the native humorists and the antiromanticism of Mark Twain, Petroleum Vesuvius Nasby, and Josh Billings, who summed it all up pretty neatly in 1868 when he said: "Americans love caustik things. . . . [They] prefer turpentine tew colone-

water . . . ." (For more on the Wiseguys, see Steve O'Donnell, page 155.)

With the underpinnings of certain discernibly American archetypes intact, American humor has inexorably evolved over the past two centuries in ways that provide insights into the history of the nation. The history of our humor is a series of seismic shifts set in motion by overwhelming forces of change—demographic revolutions, wars, the civil rights movement, and so on.

At the turn of the twentieth century, industrialization and urbanization changed the face of America; our chief humorists, hitherto rustic or western, were now urban, and

Caesar's Hour (1954–57) sketch with Sid Caesar and Nanette Fabray

Audrey Meadows and Jackie Gleason on *The Honeymooners* (1955–56)

their targets were no longer the city slicker but the country rube (although rustic humor has continued to assert itself from time to time, thanks to such comedians as Will Rogers, George Gobel, and Charlie Weaver). The modern age of humor had begun. In contrast to the old order, which valued common sense, predictability, and sanity, the new one obsessed over neuroses, psychoses, delusional behavior, and dozens of other aspects of modern psychology. (See Patricia Marx on Modern Angst, page 81.) After all, in a chaotic, irrational world, what use was common sense? Man was

hopelessly helpless in the face of technology and mind-numbing bureaucracy. This was the humor of Robert Benchley, James Thurber, and S. J. Perelman, all writers for the *New Yorker,* which made its debut in 1925 and would go on to dominate American humor for two decades.

Following World War II, another seismic shift occurred. On the surface, the America of the late forties and early fifties seemed idyllic—prosperous, homogeneous, content. Television, particularly television comedy, generally reinforced this image. The most popular comedy programs starred old-school comedians with no interest in challenging traditional values or questioning authority. Even Sid Caesar and Imogene Coca's *Your Show of Shows,* which certainly mocked postwar suburban conventions, did not have a subversive subtext, while Jackie Gleason's *The Honeymooners,* the quintessential working-class comedy, boosted the American Dream of fame and fortune rather than undermining it. (See Elvis Mitchell and Howard Rosenberg on Working-Class Stiffs, pages 51 to 71).

In truth, however, the world that had emerged from the war was profoundly different and more terrifying. This was the age of McCarthyism, with a military industrial complex spiraling out of control, and an audience that knew, in the wake of Hiroshima and Nagasaki, that nuclear annihilation was an instant away. It was only a matter of time before American comedy and television caught on.

Two comics, Mort Sahl and Lenny Bruce, led the way. Bruce assaulted America's social and religious hypocrisy; Sahl focused on political absurdities: together the two comedians pioneered a subversive school of humor that exposed the superficiality of fifties conformity, presaged the political and social tumult of the sixties, and revolutionized stand-up comedy. The comedy of Sahl, Bruce, and those who followed in their footsteps was intensely opinionated, relevant, and topical. Thanks to a 1959 article in *Time* magazine, this humor was dubbed "sick," an appellation intended to denigrate it as vulgar and perverse. In a 1962 documentary on this new humor, Amherst College professor

Mort Sahl on *Pontiac Star Parade: The Future Lies Ahead* (1959)

Lenny Bruce

Benjamin DeMott elaborated: "The sicknik addresses himself to the middle man in America. He is saying to him, 'Look, there's a great deal of meaninglessness in your life, there's a great deal of pointlessness in the things that you believe, there's a great deal of chicanery in high places, and you should be aware of this chicanery. You shouldn't sit around in a kind of euphoric state believing that everything is right with the world, that America is entirely without fault, that there isn't any hypocrisy in the church, that there isn't any indecency in the mass communications industry.' He's performing a function here, but the great question is, when the sicknik addresses himself to corruption in contemporary life, does he leave anything standing?"

Grouped with Sahl and Bruce were comedians as disparate as Bob Newhart, Jonathan Winters, Shelley Berman, and Mike Nichols and Elaine May; what all had in common was that their humor derived from the frustrations of living in a society growing more impersonal and frightening by the day. Though not sick in the cruel, sophomoric sense,

their comedy did explore the sickness of modern society.

The relationship between television and this new brand of comedy was strained from the start. As Tony Hendra points out in his book *Going Too Far*, the new humor was intrinsically antiauthority and subversive. It dealt aggressively with subjects that had hitherto been off-limits in popular comedy, challenging rather than confirming existing attitudes and assumptions. Television in the fifties and early sixties, under siege from McCarthyism, generally steered clear of threatening humor; thus, old-style comedians like Danny Thomas, Red Skelton, Jack Benny, and Jackie Gleason dominated the airwaves. Meanwhile, performers like Sahl and Bruce were often shunned, and even when booked were required to tone down their acts severely. (On a 1959 edition of the syndicated *Playboy's Penthouse*, Bruce recalled battling NBC censors during an appearance on *The Steve Allen Show* over a comic story about how Jews with tattoos are not allowed to be buried in Jewish cemeteries; Bruce lost the battle and was prohibited from telling the story on the

Elaine May and Mike Nichols

air. A few years later, Bruce had another performance yanked from Allen's Westinghouse Broadcasting Company talk show.)

Nevertheless, television (along with record albums) played a crucial role in the careers of many of the less confrontational new comedians, including Bob Newhart and Jonathan Winters, both of whom landed network comedy shows of their own during this time. Sophisticated young comedians like Nichols and May, Dick Gregory, Godfrey Cambridge, and Shelley Berman also benefited greatly from television exposure, particularly on the programs of Jack Paar, one of the most ardent supporters of the new comedy.

The tension between television and the new comedians was exacerbated as the sixties wore on. In this cataclysmic decade of social and political upheaval, the most popular comedy shows on television—including *Get Smart, The Red Skelton Hour,* and *The Jackie Gleason Show*—had nothing in common with much of the stand-up material that was being performed in nightclubs. Two shows hosted by stand-up-style teams, however, were among the most vociferous alternative voices: *The Smothers Brothers Comedy Hour* and *Rowan and Martin's Laugh-In.* Both shows trafficked in hip, irreverent humor remarkable for network television of the time. Both also revitalized television for the sixties, attracting counterculture audiences back to the medium that they had grown up with but had since abandoned as irrelevant. Of the two, *The Smothers Brothers Comedy Hour* was more subversive and biting, and it paid the price: CBS pulled the plug abruptly in 1969, after constant battles over the content of the show. Fittingly, it was a stand-up routine, by David Steinberg, that forced the final showdown. (CBS, deeming Steinberg's sermonette on Solomon and Jonah "irreverent and offensive," wanted to delete it from the show. There is considerable disagreement over whether the brothers were prepared to comply with the request: Tom and Dick maintained that they were, but in announcing the cancellation, CBS Television Network president Robert D. Wood claimed that the Smothers Brothers had breached their contract by

Nipsey Russell

failing to submit the program in time for a screening by the network and its affiliated stations.)

The upheaval of the sixties, plus the pioneering contributions of Sahl and Bruce, helped pave the way also for sweeping changes in the evolution of African-American comedy. In the late fifties, most African-American comedians were still confined to black clubs, shut out of mainstream venues by white resistance. But by the early sixties, that resistance had begun to crack. The first African-American comedians to cross over and get significant television exposure included: Timmie Rogers, who had starred in television's first black prime-time comedy show, the short-lived *Sugar Hill Times,* in 1949; Nipsey Russell, a regular on the sitcom *Car 54, Where Are You?* beginning in 1961; Slappy White and George Kirby, all of whom toned down their acts in

Godfrey Cambridge

guest appearances on comedy/variety shows. (Moms Mabley and Redd Foxx, on the other hand, did not, and thus were forced to wait several more years to enter the medium.) In turn, these pioneering black comedians blazed the trail for the next wave, people like Dick Gregory and Godfrey Cambridge, who, with their satiric assaults on racism, were bolder than their predecessors. This new wave also included Bill Cosby, whose boldness was of a different sort: his essentially color-blind monologues "let you see that being black is no different from being white or brown or whatever color," in the words of Redd Foxx.

By the seventies African-American comedians such as Foxx, Flip Wilson, and Richard Pryor were appearing on television regularly, performing emphatically black comedy that was enthusiastically embraced by audiences black and white—although not always by network executives. Pryor repeatedly ran afoul of NBC censors during *The Richard Pryor Show,* his 1977 comedy program that ran for only five weeks before constant wrangling over its content led to its demise.

Richard Pryor

Phyllis Diller

The late sixties and early seventies also saw the rise of the women's movement, which produced immediate results in stand-up comedy, both in the number of female comics and in the tone and content of their acts. Until this time, stand-up had been considered essentially a man's domain—an aggressive act unbecoming to women. Female comics were seen as threatening by both men and women, and resistance was widespread. As Lily Tomlin told the *Village Voice* in 1975: "For people to laugh . . . it's submissive. When people laugh they're vulnerable."

To overcome this resistance, female stand-ups prior to the late sixties often played dumb (like Gracie Allen) or were mercilessly self-deprecating; they ridiculed almost everything about themselves: their looks, their weight, their driving, their husbands, even their own children. "You have kids because the kids can clean, if you're smart," Joan Rivers says in one early routine on *The Carol Burnett Show*. "If they can crawl, they can dust. It's all your attitude. You tie the diaper to their legs and you throw the cookie across the room: 'Go get it, stupid.'" (See Anne Beatts on Men vs. Women, page 135.)

One of the foremost practitioners of this comedy was Totie Fields, a frequent guest on variety and talk shows during the sixties and seventies who rose to superstardom on the strength of self-disparaging jokes about her obesity. Phyllis Diller and Joan Rivers could be equally harsh on themselves, but both counterbalanced their self-deprecation with a hostility that mocked sexism and the conventional female role of housewife. Diller once joked that "the only day I enjoyed ironing was the day I accidentally put gin in the steam iron." In that sense, both are descendants of Jean Carroll, a stand-up comic from the forties and fifties. As a guest on variety shows and as the star of her own short-lived sitcom, Carroll conveyed the image of a forceful, intelligent, independent woman who, despite her husband's pleas, refused to quit working and stay home to "cook and clean and iron and run the house." ("I said, 'Why, dear? You've been doing a wonderful job.'") Another pioneering female

Joan Rivers performs at Michael's Pub in New York City

Elayne Boosler

Whoopi Goldberg

Lily Tomlin as Ernestine

LILY TOMLIN

I always made costumes and put on shows as a youngster, but show business seemed remote. I didn't even know about funny women until we got a TV set and I saw such comediennes as Bea Lillie, Lucille Ball, Imogene Coca, and Joan Davis.

Imogene Coca would do characters and different accents on Your Show of Shows. *I was so attracted to her comic striptease routine that I copied it—stole it!—when I was in college.*

My favorite Lucy routine is the one where she takes the ballet class and gets her foot stuck on the barre—and then later in the same episode she does the old vaudeville routine "Slowly I Turn . . ."

I liked Beatrice Lillie because she was different from anyone else. She had a mock elegance and would puncture it—she would wear a pillbox hat, throw her pearls around her neck, and flex her muscles.

When I was ten or eleven I watched Jean Carroll on Ed Sullivan's Toast of the Town. *She was the first woman stand-up I ever saw. She would do husband and children jokes. As a ten-year-old, my favorite line of hers was, "I'll never forget the first time I saw my husband, standing on a hill, his hair blowing in the breeze—and he too proud to run after it."*

stand-up, Jackie "Moms" Mabley, started out in the twenties and rose to stardom on the black club circuit in the forties with an aggressive act that combined bawdy humor with social satire. Elaine May also trafficked in social satire; her equal partnership with Mike Nichols in the fifties and early sixties had nothing in common with the self-deprecating humor that had played so prevalent a role in female stand-up comedy. Similarly, Lily Tomlin, who began making television appearances in the mid-sixties but broke through as a regular on *Rowan and Martin's Laugh-In* beginning in 1969, has specialized in intelligent, satirical humor featuring complex characters.

In the seventies and early eighties, as comedy clubs flourished, there was a phenomenal rise in the number of female stand-ups. Thanks to the work of the pioneering comediennes cited above, plus societal changes, the new

breed of female comic, including Elayne Boosler, Sandra Bernhard, Joy Behar, and Judy Tenuta, could be more assertive and frank. Further, they arrived on the scene just in time to take advantage of the burgeoning cable industry, which was desperate for inexpensive comedy entertainment. The mid-eighties produced yet another wave of female comics, who broke new ground with their unapologetic aggressiveness and their attacks on hypocrisy and female suppression, led by Whoopi Goldberg and Roseanne.

Political humor was energized in the early seventies by Watergate, which expanded the boundaries of acceptable satire on television even further than the Vietnam War and accompanying turmoil of the sixties. (For evidence of pre-Watergate satire, one need look no further than David Frye's savage send-ups of Lyndon Johnson and Richard Nixon.) By this time, the most important political comedian in the

Saturday Night Live's "Not Ready for Prime Time Players"—Garrett Morris, Jane Curtin, Bill Murray, Laraine Newman, Dan Ackroyd, Gilda Radner, and John Belushi

country may have been, not a baby boomer counterculturist descended from Lenny Bruce and Mort Sahl, but a mainstream midwesterner who idolized Jack Benny and Red Skelton and had risen through the ranks of television by emceeing variety and game shows—Johnny Carson. As host of *The Tonight Show* for thirty years, Carson delivered daily glosses on the nightly news—on everything from Vietnam to Contragate. His remarkably biting monologues packed all the more punch because of Carson's status as a symbol of "middle America." (For more on Carson and other political humor, see Tony Hendra and Marvin Kitman, pages 91–107.)

By the mid-seventies the nation's appetite for topically charged humor had begun to wane. The most influential

television comedy show of this time was the sketch-comedy program *Saturday Night Live*, which premiered in 1975. Although none of the original members of the Not Ready for Prime Time Players came from stand-up backgrounds, the show frequently featured stand-up comedians as guests. In the early years, Steve Martin was among the most frequent and successful hosts, celebrating a brand of nonsense comedy that had more in common with the Marx Brothers than Sahl and Bruce. Subsequently, several stand-up comedians did appear as regulars on *Saturday Night Live*, including Eddie Murphy and Billy Crystal—both specialists in character comedy who, like such comedy/variety pioneers as Red Skelton and Red Buttons, combined stand-up and sketch comedy by performing sketches based on characters from their stand-up routines. Beginning in 1985, another stand-up comedian, Dennis Miller, spent several seasons anchoring "Weekend Update," an ideal outlet for sardonic political humor.

Thanks to its phenomenal success, *Saturday Night Live* was able to expand the boundaries of permissible comedy on television. Interestingly, as Doug Hill and Jeff Weingrad recount in their book *Saturday Night: A Backstage History of Saturday Night Live,* when Richard Pryor hosted the sixth installment of the first season of the show in 1975, NBC was so terrified that Pryor would use profanity onstage that it persuaded executive producer Lorne Michaels to air the show with a five-second tape delay rather than live. Yet less than two years later, NBC actually gave Pryor his own comedy show. Although it lasted only five episodes, the mere fact that NBC had even attempted an alliance with Pryor was extraordinary; just twenty years earlier, Lenny Bruce, the fifties equivalent of Pryor in terms of controversy, had had trouble landing even guest spots on prime-time network television.

Saturday Night Live's hip irreverence sanctioned television as a legitimate form of entertainment for young people once again, just as *The Smothers Brothers Comedy Hour* and *Rowan and Martin's Laugh-In* had in the sixties; it also revitalized stand-up comedy, igniting an explosion of comedy clubs across the country. As Steve Martin told Tom Shales in a 1987 article for *Esquire*: "Comedy was dead eleven years ago. There was Richard Pryor and George Carlin, and that was it. It was post-Vietnam and pre-'76. People were very serious, and *Saturday Night Live* came along and liberated everybody."

If *Saturday Night Live* proved that hip, outrageous humor had a place on television, cable has reinforced that fact, providing stand-ups with concert-length showcases untempered by network standards of decency on programs like HBO's *On Location,* the granddaddy of the genre. The mid-seventies boom in comedy clubs came just in time for

Russell Simmons and Martin Lawrence on *Def Comedy Jam* (debuted in 1992)

the newly developing cable industry; like broadcast television in the late forties and early fifties, cable in its infancy was on the lookout for popular, inexpensive programs, and in both cases stand-up comedy fit the bill.

While old-school comedians like Joey Bishop, Henny Youngman, and Norm Crosby have all appeared on these shows, it is the younger comedians who have benefited most. For controversial comics like George Carlin and Denis Leary, cable offers unprecedented television freedom to aim their barbs at anyone and anything and to cuss to their hearts content. (In one of his best-known routines, Leary envisions an overweight, Elvis Presley-like Christ who wanders around the desert demanding cheeseburgers. Carlin not only repeated his infamous "Seven Words You Can Never Use on Television" routine on cable, he expanded on it.) Dennis Miller, a savage satirist who tempered his act on broadcast television for an ill-fated late-night talk show, resurfaced on HBO with his own program; his intense and lacerating opening comments are not so much monologues as primal screams. Martin Lawrence rose to national fame as host of *Def Comedy Jam,* HBO's notoriously blue showcase for African-American comedians; on Fox, he portrays a Jerry Lewis-like zany character in the far more mainstream

David Brenner as *Tonight Show* guest host in 1978

sitcom *Martin*. (For more on Tough Guys, see Mel Watkins, page 145.)

Ironically, in light of the freedom that cable offers, so many of today's most popular stand-ups have nothing in common with the smoking relevance of Carlin or the raunchiness of Lawrence. Jerry Seinfeld, Paul Reiser, Ellen DeGeneres, David Letterman, and Jay Leno are practitioners of a comedy commonly called referential, or observational, described by Tom Shales as "sardonic commentary on the passing scene—not current events, politicians, minority straits, social crises, but the everyday trivia of modern life." (See Douglas Coupland on The Observationalist, page 109.) Typically, these comedians joke about pop culture (particularly television), relationships, and their own youths; they obsess over everyday exigencies like trying to remember where you've parked your car, or what happens to socks that

get lost in the laundry. They recall James Thurber's famous definition of a humorist: "He talks largely about small matters and smally about great affairs."

Shales and others have traced the dominance of this brand of comedy to the Reagan years, when baby boomers were transmogrified into yuppies and, desperate to bury the anxiety and disillusionment of the sixties and early seventies, began to crave comedy that reassured rather than threatened, amused rather than provoked.

Although predominantly outward-oriented, today's representational comedy does include a narcissistic strain of humor about growing up, childhood, and lost innocence that is essentially a soft-core version of the sophisticated, intensely personal comedy that Woody Allen and Bill Cosby pioneered in Greenwich Village nightclubs thirty years ago, at a time when many of their colleagues were more concerned with social or political relevance. Their enormously

Robert Klein in a 1983 appearance on *Late Night with David Letterman* (1982–93)

Woody Allen on *The Tonight Show Starring Johnny Carson*

influential work inspired a generation of nostalgia comedians like Robert Klein, David Brenner, and Rita Rudner, who drew from the same well—the traumas of childhood and adolescence—and then expanded into shared memories of insignificant pop culture icons, like Pop Tarts and the board game "Clue."

Allen has often opined that modern men and women obsess over trivial matters because weightier ones—death, disease, and the randomness of evil—are so frightening and unmanageable that it is impossible to acknowledge them without the risk of utter personal devastation. Perhaps,

then, today's observational comedians are only doing what comedians have always done, enriching us with laughter, the ultimate escape—not from truth, for comedians are the Diogenes of our time, but from despair. As that noted American stand-up comedian Abraham Lincoln once said, "I laugh because I must not cry."

On the other hand, maybe not. Maybe all that laughter—elicited by thousands of stand-up comedians since the dawn of time—comes down to nothing more, as Robert Benchley once wrote, than a "compensatory reflex to take the place of sneezing."

WORKING-CLASS STIFFS

Black and White and Blue

by Elvis Mitchell

The Mary Tyler Moore Show (1970–77)

Working class in TV comedy has always meant exhibiting anger. Even as Mary Richards unfurled her twittery WASPish neuroses—anguish with a hint of jasmine —Lou Grant lumbered through the newsroom, furry forearms visible from beneath his rolled-up sleeves and (grunt!) refusing to floss between meals. (For a very long time on TV, the working class was always represented with rolled-up sleeves, someone's conception of wardrobe from the Salt of the Earth Collection for Botany 500.) Grant, even by virtue of being white-collar working class, brought the plainspoken attitude of the blue-collar to sitcoms. And he was a part of a revitalization that began in the seventies, when stand-up comedians used blue-collar bluntness to communicate with audiences.

The best of blue-collar comedy works almost conceptually, and by the best, I mean what came after—and in response to—the river of eager-to-please sludge that passed for comedy in the sixties, as uninteresting as the gray welcome mats that decorated the front stoops of the upper-middle-class castles of *Father Knows Best, Leave It to Beaver, Bewitched,* and *The Donna Reed Show.* The series that came in their wake made ironic mention of their tapioca predecessors; the characters on the working-class shows seemed to idealize a vision of Barbara Billingsley pouring glasses of fresh lemonade, making her seem as if she were a serving girl on *Fantasy Island.* And until the triumph of *Roseanne,* the distemper always grew from being frozen out of the middle class. Even that dream has been denied Roseanne and Dan Conner, and much of the show's humor comes from their attempting to make peace with this condition. (In fact, shaking hands with the suavely grinning Mr. Roarke is a more likely tableau than the Conners making their way into the bourgeoisie.)

Roseanne offers the lesson that shows shouldn't be judged based on their first seasons. At the beginning, Roseanne stood behind the couch like a first base umpire, snarling a barrage of all-purpose jokes that grew out of the household goddess routine that she had refined at comedy clubs. What we may have assumed was limited talent was actually the result of Roseanne's slamming into the wall of inflexibility she was offered by the show's executive producer and "creator" Matt Williams. (It's rumored she had him run off the show on a rail; presumably, no tar and feathers were available.)

She was right. Her complaints, as shrill as they may have sounded, were well reasoned. The show was about her voice, not just the standard back-and-forth of

Jackie Gleason and Art Carney on
The Honeymooners (1955–56)

Roseanne (debuted in 1988)

gags, however professional, that the best sitcom can offer. Her understanding of
a need to create tension—a basic tenet of drama as well as a result of her shrewd
provocateur's instinct—resonates throughout. *Roseanne*, which has one of the best
casts in the history of television, is often about coping with unhappiness that spills
over into several episodes and is never completely mopped up; real, decent people
who are constantly pissed off, and can never really explain why. (To see what she
was railing against—becalmed, standard sitcom fare—take a look at *Home
Improvement* or the short-lived *Thunder Alley*, where the aforementioned Williams
rules with an Iron La-Z-Boy. You can also point to the unusual evolution of the
Roseanne characters over the run of the series.) However, the show hasn't completely
divorced itself from the conventions of sitcom; the star still rules.

The outsized presences that inhabited blue-collar comedy grew out of the
fact that many of the stars seemed to be growing out of their clothes, and had half-
baked ambitions to match their appetites. Intriguingly, the shows featured performers who had lived through rough and tumble adventures in show business
and life; their world views and energy overtook the shows. In *Sanford and Son*,

Demond Wilson and Redd Foxx in *Sanford and Son* (1972–77)

I used to be poor but no more. I mean p-o-o-o-o-o-o-o-o-o-o-o-o-o-o-o-r. Yes, I came from a big family. Eleven kids in my family—eleven. We lived in a one-room kitchenette. I used to come home early so I could sleep on top. Christmas of 1932, my Daddy went out in the alley and shot the rifle, and came back in the house and told all the kids Santa Claus just committed suicide.

Redd Foxx
ABC Stage 67: *"A Time for Laughter,"* 1967

Redd Foxx took his family surname, Sanford, and had it used as the character's name. At the very least, this increased his emotional investment in the show. On *Sanford and Son*, Fred Sanford conjured get-rich-quick-schemes: he dreamed of enjoying the easy life, of drinking a big chilled jelly jar full of Ripple sitting on a lawn chair on an actual lawn instead of the dusty, grassless knoll in front of his house.

Before the show went on the air, Foxx was known mostly to the black community as a sly crank who danced around profanity, and sometimes used it in his stand-up routine; at best, his jokes could be summarized as powder blue. It was only much later in his career that he went from risqué to profane. His showbiz migratory pattern was probably tagged and followed by *Sanford* producers Norman Lear and Bud Yorkin after Foxx's appearance in the blaxploitation film *Cotton Comes to Harlem*, in which he played an amiable junkman. But it quickly became clear that Foxx, who had been in the entertainment business for nearly thirty years by that time, wasn't going to be turned into a smiley Negro totem. He brought along a group of young comics and observers to staff his show, among them Richard Pryor. Much of the first season of the show has the tough-minded tang of their stand-up material. An episode in which Sanford finds himself in traffic court gleams with a gem I'm sure Pryor fished from his own work; a group of mostly black defendants moving through the judicial system prompts Sanford to bark, "That's what they mean by justice. Just us! Last time I saw this many niggers, it was in a Tarzan movie." (Pryor was credited as a cowriter of the episode.)

Foxx's Sanford has the deftness and ease that grew logically out of a comedian's performing confidence. Foxx's own anger became a kind of public tantrum, as his foot-stamping demands for a rehearsal space with windows, and other peevish behavior got more attention than the show itself, which was a shame. He deserved better. *Sanford* turned out to be an act of sheer will for Foxx, possibly the apotheosis of his career; it seems to me he was certainly never as good before or after, in the way that only series TV often allows a performer to be, who realizes he has one defining opportunity to seize. *Chico and the Man*, starring self-described "Hunga-Rican" stand-up Freddie Prinze, was so close in form to *Sanford* that I almost wanted to dust it for Lear's fingerprints. *Chico* was set in an East L.A. auto repair shop and featured a young Latino man dealing with his curmudgeonly father figure. But *Chico* came from producer James Komack, who also snatched the furry Gabe Kaplan and stuck him in front of John Travolta in *Welcome Back, Kotter*. Both *Kotter* and *Chico* featured stars who snuggled up to the hearts of the country; unlike *Sanford*, these shows seemed breezy and cheerfully artificial. (Only later would we discover that the tortured Prinze was deeply unhappy.)

Lamont: Do you think I'm gonna stay in this ridiculous business all my life? I'm going on to bigger and better things.

Fred: Like what?

Lamont: Like . . . like shipbuilding.

Fred: Shipbuilding!

Lamont: Yeah, that's right, shipbuilding. With what I know about iron and steel, man, I could become a millionaire, just like that Greek cat that married Jackie Kennedy. And you know something? He started out poor, just like me.

Fred: Only one difference.

Lamont: What's that?

Fred: He started out a Greek.

Redd Foxx
Sanford and Son, *1972*

Jack Albertson and Freddie Prinze on *Chico and the Man* (1974–78)

Freddie Prinze

You take something simple, like asking what time it is, you know. Like down South, they're very proud: "Do you know the time?" "Hell, yes. Granddaddy gave me this watch—solid gold—seventy years old. It's, uh . . . (looking at watch) it's 3:30 or 9 o'clock." You ask black people, "Do you know what time it is?" "Do I look like Big Ben to you, sucka?" You ask one of my people, "You know what time it is?" (opening up his jacket) "You wanna buy a watch, man?"

Freddie Prinze
On Location: Freddie Prinze and Friends
1976

Chico: You need me.

The Man: For what?

Chico: I'm Super Mex.

The Man: Who's Super Mex?

Chico: Super Mexicani. Ask anyone in the barrio about Chico Rodriguez, you know what they tell you? "Oh, yeah, Chico can take apart an engine and put it back together blindfolded. He don't need no fancy machine to tell him what the trouble is." (pointing to his ear) This is my fancy machine: one listen, I know what the trouble is. I take care of my uncle's '64 Chevy, beautiful condition—pom-poms on all the antennas, cellophane seat covers, right? Little dog in the back window with the head keep going up and down.

The Man: Here (handing him a wrench).

Chico: You want me to fix something?

The Man: Yeah, tighten up your tongue before it flaps out of your mouth.

Freddie Prinze
Chico and the Man, *1974*

Another Lear/Yorkin show of the era with a mostly black cast, *Good Times*, also featured a stand-up, Jimmie Walker. But the show wasn't informed by his point-of-view. Walker was used as spice, stalking the tiny apartment of his impoverished family like an arthritic preying mantis, and sprinkling his "Dyn-O-Mites" liberally throughout the we-so-po' tedium. The show was a generally self-pitying affair that employed the tried-and-true Scream Theater tactic that Lear probably had a patent out on. (The families on his shows bellowed at each other so much that the noise showed up on weather-radar maps.) But even *Good Times* offered a brittle vividness that had been lacking in situation comedies before it hit the scene, spinning out of *All in the Family*'s orbit.

Taxi (1978–83) with Judd Hirsch and Danny DeVito

The most fascinating thing about the working-class series that reinvigorated television was that instead of using a character such as Lou Grant as a single low comedy foil—a shot of B-12 to burn away some of the overly self-aware politeness—we were offered entire households full of them. Lear recognized that bigger-than-life protagonists who were totally unapologetic had far more to offer than did the suburban families who mouthed wisecracks by the yard. So, he set about changing that.

The first of the working class to slam a door open in the seventies, after several years of drought that started when Ralph Kramden handed out his last Madison Avenue transfer, was Carroll O'Connor's character Archie Bunker. With his heavy-lidded stare and contempt for everything that didn't jibe with what "Richard E. Nixon" was selling, Bunker, as conceived by O'Connor and Norman Lear, was a baleful earful. Like *Sanford*, which it preceded, *All in the Family* was based on a show that had achieved great success in England. (Irony abounds; the working-class shows that changed the face of American sitcoms came from the land that gave us Oscar Wilde and James Bond. Yikes!)

Like Foxx, O'Connor was an actor who had kicked around for some time, and his battles with Lear became, if not the stuff of legend, then the filler on the pages of the *National Enquirer*. Like Foxx and Roseanne, he was trying to give his character weight, and they all came through with a dignity and awareness unusual for such animals. Instead of being impaled on one-liners, what these performers and producers did elevated the form.

What Lear and his partners also did, willingly or not, generated incredible excitement, especially since at the same time, the low-key proficiency of the MTM stable was cranking out the stylized workplace comedies that were firmly planted in the middle class. So when Jim Brooks, seemingly inspired by Lear's example, tried to fashion a recombinant hybrid in *Taxi*, which attempted to merge the middle-class forbearance of MTM shows with the shining-eyed yearning of the blue-collar, the mix was sometimes bewildering. With the exception of Judd Hirsch's Alex Rieger, the others all had dreams of escaping the bonds of taxi-driverdom and becoming something better—actor, gallery owner, and in Tony Danza's case, star of his own sitcom—and Rieger accepted his fate with a nonchalance that bordered on bemused European fatalism. In the end, it was dispatcher Louie DePalma, all hot-tempered simplicity and nerviness, who impressed most. He was pure working man, right down to his rolled-up shirt sleeves. Lou Grant woulda' been proud.

Nowadays, it's Brett Butler who continues the tradition of blue-collar stand-up that has been so successful for most of her forebears. Her show, *Grace Under*

Carroll O'Connor and Rob Reiner in *All in the Family* (1971–78)

Jimmie Walker and Freddie Prinze join Mike Douglas (at left) on *The Mike Douglas Show* (1963–82)

Ellen DeGeneres

Fire, seems to have clipped a few coupons from Roseanne's book. Butler's Grace, an oil refinery worker and single mother of three, doesn't seem to live under fire. Rather, she spits fire. Butler's redneck perspective, blue-collar anguish, and white-knuckle existence comes too close to the reality of Roseanne, but lacks the specific honesty that Roseanne has managed to turn into an empire.

The 1995 entry for the stand-up comedian to make the move into stand-up sitcom is Ellen DeGeneres. DeGeneres has actually stepped back to the moist-palmed WASPy world of Mary Tyler Moore, with a head of blonde hair that seems Zestfully clean and a pair of worried blue eyes. (No wonder, since her show has undergone more changes than Roseanne has personalities.) Following the lead of *Seinfeld*, *Ellen* would have you think that the bracing blue-collar outrage is being bred out of stand-ups in situation comedy. Well, think again. I'm sure this is only the calm before the storm.

Ralph, Roseanne, and Grace:
Color Their Collars Blue

by Howard Rosenberg

We're all blinded by color spots occasionally. To me, a lily white-collar, for example, blue-collar is what you do in Los Angeles before you sell your first script or join the cast of a soap opera or become the lead story on *Entertainment Tonight*. It's also hair nets stretched across plastic rollers. It's babies, beer, and beer bellies. It's Laundromats and Roller Derby. It's a pack of cigarettes rolled up in the sleeve of a T-shirt. It's Harleys, leather boots, and tattoos of babes with big boobs. It's fuzzy dice hanging from the rearview mirror of a '56 Chevy.

I don't have to be told that these are stereotypes, and that a blue-collar reading this might want to hang my fuzzy dice from his rearview mirror. But lives are compartmentalized, and my blue-collar compartment would fit into a coin slot. I did spend my adolescent summers in a toy factory. My *dad's* toy factory. Apart from television characters, the only people of blue-collar persuasion that I have even semiregular contact with are our gardener and the man who paints our house from time to time. The gardener speaks no English. That leaves the painter. His name is Jeff.

"Jeff," I asked on the phone, "do you and your family watch much TV?"

"Not a lot."

What? They're not laser-locked on that supreme blue-collar comedy, *Roseanne*?

"Never watch it," he said.

Or that smash blue-collar comedy, *Grace Under Fire*?

"Not interested," he said.

He had only a fuzzy impression of junk-dealing *Sanford and Son* and didn't give a hoot for reruns of bus-driving Ralph Kramden in *The Honeymooners*, or his sewage-sloshing foil, Ed Norton.

"Not my taste," Jeff said.

Just what did his blue-collar family's tastes run to on TV? I tried not to sound *too* condescending. "My kids like to watch MTV," he said. I pictured his kids being Beavis and Butthead.

Jeff added: "And I kind of like *NYPD Blue*."

Why was that? Jeff paused—I figured he was removing his toothpick and lighting a Camel before delivering his professorial response. "There's something primal about watching cops."

Something pri...

One of these days, Jeff. One of these days—POW—right to the moon! I'm certain

John Goodman and Roseanne
on *Roseanne*

now that Jeff's collar is azure and that he finds *me* primal. After all, I'm the one who's TV-driven, and when it comes to the blue-collar comedy of stand-up comics, I'm the one who's sold on Brett Butler's *Grace Under Fire* and Roseanne's *Roseanne*, thinks well of *Sanford and Son,* and still marvels at Jackie Gleason's enduring tour de force, *The Honeymooners.* Although I write for the *Los Angeles Times,* I rarely watch *Dave's World,* the CBS comedy series based on the life of newspaper columnist Dave Barry. Thus, why would I assume that Jeff or anyone else making his living from manual labor would necessarily warm to comedies depicting a blue-collar crowd? No less, one that in some cases is tailored to the perceptions of *white*-collars.

I'm full of Jewish angst over the narrowness implicit in my lingering acceptance of working-class stereotypes (I forgot to mention billed caps with farm machinery logos). But thanks to TV, for the first time since *All in the Family* and other working-class sitcoms of the seventies, I am inching my way into the realm of blue-collardom as expressed by several popular comedies.

It's not surprising that so many stand-up comics have spread to sitcoms, given that most such shows have always been oriented toward the one-liners that nourish the club acts of comedians. Correspondingly, there's a logical link even between blue-collars and blue comics. After all, stand-up comics are like spot welders, remaining in one place while doing repetitive work. So why wouldn't some of them spill over to blue-collar sitcoms?

This stand-up/sitcom connection is not new. The seventies brought grinning Jimmie Walker fifteen minutes of "Dyn-O-Mite!" in the Chicago projects as the often-jobless J. J. of *Good Times.* Freddie Prinze was "lookin' *go-o-o-d*" for a time as the East L.A. barrio-kid-turned-garage worker in *Chico and the Man.* And Redd Foxx's endearing junk dealer in *Sanford and Son* made ghetto life fun . . . for non-ghetto viewers. The lives of Foxx's Fred Sanford and Demond Wilson's Lamont Sanford were strewn with farcical crises, and their yard and house were strewn with junk. "If you'll just be patient," that aging martyr Fred assured Lamont in the premiere, "I'll be gone soon—and all this'll be yours." It was charming rubbish.

When it came to stand-ups in working-class comedies, though, young comics Walker and Prinze seemed less like permanent residents than transients pausing before moving on to new gigs. And the veteran Foxx's junkman was so broad that his shabby environment appeared as stagy as the illness that he regularly faked to make Lamont feel sorry for him. In contrast, there's something indelible about the blue-collarism of the earlier Gleason and today's Butler and Roseanne.

Roseanne and Butler are soul partners in that both use their ABC comedies to satirize the social forces that buffet ordinary Americans of every stripe.

Esther Rolle and Jimmie Walker on *Good Times* (1974–79)

Jackie Gleason on *The Honeymooners*
(1955–56)

*Alice: Ralph why can't we have a television
set? The Nortons are on their second one,
we haven't even had our first one yet. Why
do you always have to be so cheap?*

*Ralph: Cheap? Cheap! Is that why you
think I won't get you a set? 'Cos I'm cheap?
Well, that shows how much you know.*

Alice: Well, what is the reason?

*Ralph: D'you wanna know the reason?
You wanna know the reason? The reason?
Alright, I'll tell you the reason. I'm waiting
for 3-D television. That's the reason.*

Jackie Gleason
The Honeymooners, *1955*

Although you could infer what you wished from the drab lives of the Kramdens and Nortons, their thick cocoon of urban squalor on *The Honeymooners* appeared hermetically sealed from outside influence. And Gleason wasn't into preaching.

Roseanne's and Butler's series also differ from Gleason's in that they perpetuate the sardonic stand-up comedy personae that earned both stars their TV deals. No stand-up, no sitcom. Gleason, on the other hand, was reputedly not much of a monologuist, even though he dabbled at stand-up comedy in the infancy of his career. What he was, as Americans were to learn, was a brilliantly gifted sketch comic whose own growth paralleled that of TV and whose most gleaming creation, that blowhard Ralph, lived in a state of deprivation not unlike Gleason's own poverty as a kid growing up with his mother at 328 Chauncey Street in Brooklyn. It's no coincidence, obviously, that the crumbly Brooklyn tenement where the Kramdens and Nortons lived (if that was living) was given the same address.

What defines the blue-collar characters in these comedies?

——*Where They Live.* Next to Ralph, Gleason's most memorable character was that boozy millionaire playboy Reginald Van Gleason III, who, after one whiff of the Kramden's two-room walk-up, would have rolled his eyes and said: "Mmmboy, are you poor!"

Poor surely, even by bus-driver standards, despite Ralph's constant get-rich schemes from glow-in-the-dark wallpaper to his KranMar's Delicious Mystery Appetizer, which turned out to be dog food. Although Ralph's ambition was as epic as his paunch, the Kramdens' home front was like a bleak slum, the difference being that slum dwellers generally have a TV set and a permanent phone. The Kramdens didn't. Their main room contained a round wood table with a red-and-white checked tablecloth, an old dresser, and a tiny icebox next to an old stove and a battered sink. To the left was a bedroom that we never saw but could envision Ralph and Alice sleeping on a rollaway.

When it comes to physical comforts, compared with the Kramdens, Grace and the Conners *are* Reggie Van Gleason III. Although to Grace the antique rental house that she and her kids occupy is a "leaky piece of crap," it looks pretty swell for someone of her means. And the Conners, too, are relatively comfortable, if cramped, inside their modest tract house.

It helped when their older daughter and her husband finally moved out. When they did, in the seventh season, it was to a trailer park, where one of their trashy neighbors (a cameo by Sharon Stone) mistook Dan and Roseanne for residents. Asking the Conners if they owned their mobile home drew this mocking quip from Roseanne: "Whaddaya think, we're made of money? We rent!"

Gleason is joined by Julie Andrews on *The Jackie Gleason Show* (1952–70)

Remember the good old days when you could go all the way to the Bronx on the subway for five cents? Today you can't even call the Bronx on the phone for five cents. Used to walk into a butcher shop and buy a pound of chopped meat, and he'd throw in a big hunk of liver; he says, "This is for your cat." What chance you got today? Liver is so expensive there isn't a cat in the country can afford to eat liver. Money means nothing. You tell a girl today she looks like a million? She smacks you right in the snoot.

Jackie Gleason
Jackie Gleason and His American Scene
Magazine, *1964*

Sandra Bernhard, Laurie Metcalf, and Roseanne, on *Roseanne*

——*What They Do for a Living.* Look at that face and body, listen to that mouth, the entire package evoking the obnoxious passengers, snarly motorists, and gridlock that have brought Ralph Kramden to a boil. He drags himself home buckling from the baggage of his day behind the wheel, irritated and fed up, a human tinderbox just waiting for a match. Inevitably, that match is his wife, Alice, whether Pert Kelton (the first Alice) or Audrey Meadows.

A dreamer, Ralph's overstatement and delusions of grandeur extended to his job. "I don't think you were ever in love with me," he snapped at Alice during one of their spats. "You were just in love with my uniform."

And who else would be Ralph's best friend but Art Carney's guileless Norton, a self-anointed "underground engineer" who didn't know much, but did know that the best way to get across town during rush hour was to "go by sewer."

Three decades later, Roseanne Conner was introduced to viewers as a whiny, wisecracking slob of a blob, a mother of three in Lanford, Illinois, where she worked in a plastics factory, then in a beauty shop, then in a restaurant as a waitress, and now owns a diner with her sister, Jackie. As a bonus, she's become one of the nation's rare blue-collar moms with a face job.

When we first met her big-bellied husband, Dan, he was a building contractor who once boasted of being the "drywall master of the universe." The recession hit the Conners hard, though, and John Goodman's Dan now works in city maintenance alongside his son-in-law and brother-in-law, blue-collar being the family business. The job is a drag.

Roseanne: "Dan, how was work today?"

Dan: "Well, today was a special one for me. It was the 179th day in a row where I did exactly the same thing."

Although the view through Roseanne-colored glasses is distinctly working class, it's Butler's Grace Kelly who is TV's Rosie the Riveter. She, too, is a mother of three (although disclosing that as a teenager she had a fourth child who was put up for adoption). But unlike the happily married Roseanne Conner, Grace is a divorced Alabaman, who walked out on her "knuckle-draggin', cousin-lovin', beersuckin' redneck" of a husband, who beat her.

Grace works at a CBD oil refinery where her hard hat and coveralls identify her as one of the guys. Almost. Some of her funniest moments there come at the expense of her dimmest male colleagues whom she tolerates and good-naturedly mocks, pretending she's an anthropologist and they're *Gorillas in the Mist.* Although well-meaning, these are mostly human bricks who regard all women as "chicks," greet a new female employee with "hubba hubba," and are so thick, Grace notes, that they think "harass is two words."

Roseanne

Roseanne on a job interview:

Employer: Can you start tomorrow?

Roseanne: Why?

Employer: 'Cos I need someone to start tomorrow."

Roseanne: Well, I don't even know if I'm going to take this job.

Employer: You have to take this job, you're the only one who applied.

Roseanne: I would just kind of like to think about it.

Employer: Think about what? If it's that miserable you either quit or I unload you.

Roseanne: Well, as long as there's some humiliation at the end of the tunnel.

Roseanne
Roseanne, 1990

I'm a housewife. I never get out of the house. I sit at home all the time; I never do anything. I hate that word. I prefer to be called Domestic Goddess, after all it's more descriptive.

Roseanne
Funny, 1984

Brett Butler

On our wedding day my ex-husband got in a fist fight with the accordion player because the poor guy didn't know any Led Zeppelin. That was my first hint that maybe I'd chosen unwisely. Anyway, after eight years and three children, I decided to go it alone, and believe me, it was the hardest decision I've ever made. But I figured I had two choices: I could spend the rest of my life waking up next to a knuckle-draggin', cousin-lovin', beer-suckin' red-neck, or I could work like a dog for lousy money while I raise three kids all by myself. Boy, is it nice to have choices.

Brett Butler
Grace Under Fire, 1993

——*What They Carry.* The rule of thumb here is that white-collars go out for lunch, blue-collars don't. That means high visibility in these sitcoms for that laborer's attaché, the old lunch bucket, one of which sits atop Ralph's dresser like a trophy, another of which appears to be a permanent extension of Dan Conner's hand. Plus, it's no accident that Roseanne's diner is named the Lanford Lunch Box.

——*What They Do for Recreation.* Bowling. Ralph Kramden did it, the Conners do it. When it's time to bond with TV, though, males on *Roseanne* sink into a sofa in front of the set, remote control in one hand, can of beer in the other. They lap up manly camaraderie to the extent that Roseanne observed in one episode that all guys want "is another hairy person to itch and have chips with."

——*What They Say.* Social class is defined in part by language. As soon as he opened his mouth, you knew immediately that Ralph was not a graduate of NYU. But even he was an elegant silk stocking compared with coarse, lewd, English-butchering Roseanne, who never met an "ain't" or double negative she didn't like.

On her mouth and boorishness alone, Roseanne Conner would qualify for a spot on one of those daytime talk shows whose guests communicate like howler monkeys and represent their alien subcultures by calling each other names. You can just see Roseanne on the panel, having great, cackling fun, her caustic put-downs soaring over the heads of her fellow guests and the host.

Grace, on the other hand, demolishes stereotypes by virtue of her standing in the proletariat literati. Whereas a bestial quality defines Roseanne's high intelligence, Grace is braininess with a bookmark. She's as apt to mention master painter Raphael as Sally Jessy Raphaël. As Butler has noted about her series, "This isn't just making Tuna Helper on TV." It's true that Grace once thought she saw Elvis. Blame that on her genes. But slipped into her own caustic asides are also such names as Freud and book titles as *Lord of the Flies*, and in trying to balance the juggernauts of mother and shift worker, she worries about her life becoming more "gothic and obscure."

Not that she chases pretensions. When Grace demands a "public apology from God for wasting my life," she's not entirely serious. And when a company shrink chides her for working at the refinery, her response is not to bask in his praise of her intelligence but to question *his* employment there.

Grace, Roseanne, and Ralph are all there, in effect, as the grandest of stand-up comedy's blue-collar bunch, and primal white-collars are the better for it. Mmm-boy, are they good!

Dave Thomas and Brett Butler on *Grace Under Fire* (debuted in 1993)

Shared Anger

by Denis Leary

All comics have in common the gift of social commentary. Even Steve Martin at his silliest makes us laugh because we know—from our developed social skills—how ridiculous it is for a grown man to wear a fake arrow on his head in public. But the group of names gathered here may be the most specifically adept at throwing this world's everyday hypocrisy back in our faces. All of us tend to shake our heads at the inane rules and regulations of daily life, but these voices inflate and examine them to the point of hysteria.

As with all great comedy, it's hard to throw off the thrill of a great piece of material that not only dissects an issue you've been angry about but also makes you laugh your ass off. I remember the thrill I felt as a kid when my friends and I piled into Tommy Sullivan's apartment and listened to George Carlin's comedy album *Class Clown* for the first time while Tommy's parents were at work.

We laughed so hard our testicles dropped.

Of course, Carlin's routine "Seven Words You Can Never Use on Television" had us in hysterics, and we only laughed harder because they were words we hadn't heard on a record before. But some twenty-five years later, that piece of material has become a touchstone for social commentary in the world of stand-up comedy. Not because it saddles the issue with the weight of satire, which it does. Not because it explains the issue in a pointed and visceral way, which it does. But because it is funny. Even today. That's the thin line comics walk when dealing with social satire: lean a millimeter too far in the wrong direction and you may find yourself lecturing.

Toward the end of his life, Lenny Bruce—legal briefs in hand and sweat staining his ample brow—found it necessary to take his obscenity case to the public. His final performances were full of keen social commentary wrapped in his new-found knowledge of the law. The laughs may have diminished, but he wasn't looking for laughs anymore.

At that point he just wanted to air out the instrument in front of a jury of his peers—the audience. And still it was fascinating. And still the funny moments would have you wiping your eyes. The best work from the best comics tends to do that, and to stand the test of time. Alan King's anger and frustration with the airline industry sounds as if his luggage got lost yesterday when, in fact, the material was developed over thirty years ago. A lot of the airline material heard in comedy clubs on a nightly basis in the nineties is just a cheap rehash of the gold King mined way back when.

Dick Gregory

We're making progress. Twenty years ago the light-complected Negro had it made; today it's the dark-complected Negro. Simply because of government contracts. In order for big business to get good government contracts today, they have to hire Negro and white on an equal basis. So they go out and get the blackest cat they can find. So when that government inspector walks in that plant he can see him seven blocks away. "So you got one!" "Darn right, we have one."

Dick Gregory
The Steve Allen Show, 1963

People start screaming in the suburbs, "Back to Africa with 'em, back to..." I said, "Back to Africa with who?" Shit, I ain't never been to Africa. You wanna send me home, send me to St. Louis, Missouri, 4461 Enright, top floor. Africa, what the hell I look like standing in the jungle with a $750 mohair suit and some alligator shoes?

Redd Foxx
On Location, 1978

DICK GREGORY

My comedic influence came from radio, not television. By the time television came out, I had already been influenced by white comedians on the radio. In my day, the black comedians such as Rochester and Mantan Moreland were the only black comics we heard, but nobody wanted to emulate them, including me. Since I had no interest in emulating them, the only other comedians I heard were white comedians on the radio, such as Bob Hope. So I would say one of the comedians that had an influence on my career was Bob Hope. I would listen to Bob Hope on the radio doing his first three minutes of genius out of the paper, and then into that Ma and Pa stuff. His first three minutes were always topical.

Mort Sahl was one of the most influential comics out there. He was an intellect, not a genius. I looked around and there was Lenny Bruce, the few times he was on television, he was a genius. So I had one white comic over here, he's more intellectual than me; another white comic over there, he's a genius; so I go back to Bob Hope. So here I was inside a black body, influenced by white men in my head.

Bill Cosby and Richard Pryor, they couldn't influence me, because I came before them. My mind was white, but my delivery was colored. I was no threat to nobody at all! I was still the slave master's servant. That's what they heard when I got on the stage. That's why they gave me credit for being so brilliant, because they couldn't believe that anybody could sound so colored, because I was sounding colored, with a white man's mind. I learned math and all the fine things you learn in college, except English. And until this day, I don't like English; I don't understand it, I don't care about it and that's what kept my head free.

So when television hit, my thing was already formulated. I didn't even want to look at the comedians on television. I would look at Bob Hope for the first few minutes, until he gets into his slapstick, which didn't move me at all. I looked at the white comics for a rhythm, then the black comics came around with an all new rhythm; and the whole rhythm changed.

His hilarious "Survived by His Wife" routine, in which he reads aloud onstage obituaries he's plucked from various newspapers over the years, will be funny well into Judgment Day because it is based on a cold, hard, irreversible fact—women outlive men. These bits are immortal. They arrive gleaming and stand strong as a steel tree. Almost ageless. Carlin's "Stuff" routine is so eternal he reprises it in front of live audiences today, and they applaud as if the Stones had just finished "Satisfaction." The same can be said for his "Football/Baseball" bit.

Lenny Bruce's "Religions, Inc." has perhaps more validity today than it did three-and-a-half decades ago. His comments on racism and white insecurity—so aptly captured in the album *How to Relax Your Colored Friends at Parties*—still ring very true.

Lenny Bruce

Little Rock has solved the (integration) sit-uation; they've done it through legislation. If the colored people can pass the literacy test they get to vote. And it's very fair: (with Southern accent) "Well, let's see now, line all the colored people up here, and if they pass the test they get to vote here. It's very easy, you just sign your name. Here's this ball point pen, this piece of wax paper . . . ."

Lenny Bruce
Playboy's Penthouse, *1959*

George Carlin

CATHY LADMAN

When I'm old and wrinkled, this is the story I will tell most often about my stand-up career.

Wait a second. I am old and wrinkled.

When I was about eight years old, I began listening to the comedy albums my parents owned. There were only a few. There was Vaughn Meader's First Family; *there was* Nichols and May Examine Doctors. *That's the one I listened to most often. I would put it on the record player, sit in front of the speaker, and listen to that album over and over and over. I memorized every single band. I knew all of the parts; I did all of the characters. I don't even know if I knew it was funny, but I was incredibly drawn to it. In fact, every night, when I was going to bed, my mother would come into my room to hear me say my prayers, which I would follow with a selection from the album. She would say something like, "That's very nice, dear," and then she probably ran frantically to her Dr. Spock manual, hoping that she would find some explanation for this deviance.*

She didn't. And I became a comedian.

In 1989, I was in my apartment, getting ready to do my very first appearance on The Tonight Show. *I thought I'd put on some music so I could sing and work with all the adrenaline that was pumping through my system. And, all of a sudden, it occurred to me to put on* Nichols and May Examine Doctors. *And there I was, about to fulfill a comedian's dream by going on* The Tonight Show, *and listening to the very thing that first inspired me.*

It was one of the sweetest moments of my life.

I've heard it argued that for comedians the hardest part of growing old is trying to stay vital, not losing that cynical edge, that spark of anger and energy that makes the hair stand up on the nape of your neck, kicks your synapses into place, opens your jaw, and lets the words fly out. I think the so-called social commentators have a leg up on this level of life. I've seen King and Klein at work up close in recent years—neck muscles straining up to blood-red faces as they jab the air about Clinton, Cuba, cancer, casseroles, and so forth. I've seen George Carlin kill several hundred brain cells barking about antiabortion activists. These are sure signs of a die-hard social commentator. They care too much. So, they carry on carping. Angry. Alive.

They will not go gentle into that good night.

Any time white people wanna smooth some shit over they go get that rich nigger. Put you on TV, to represent the people, you know. They ask you questions like, "Damon, now that you've made this thirteen million dollars—and we're not counting—now that you've made all this money, let me ask you this, let me just throw this out at you, you respond any way you want . . . Is there racism in America?" You be sittin' there thinkin' 'bout that paycheck, talkin' 'bout, "No Suh. . . If 'n they is, I ain't seen none."

Damon Wayans
The Last Stand?, *1991*

So, if there is any information in the information superhighway that will help us as a society, then I'm all for it. If there is information that will show us how to do away with skinheads, and MTV, and the grunge culture, and slasher movies, and adults who use the word "goes" instead of "said," and millionaire celebrities who wear torn jeans on television, and people who say the Holocaust never took place, and drug dealers, and last, and by all means least, the National Rifle Association, then I am all for it. But if the information on the information superhighway is only about movies, and clogging the lines with the unedited thoughts of millions of lonely little guys hunched over their computers in lieu of having any semblance of a life, then show me the off-ramp on the information superhighway.

Mark Russell
Mark Russell Comedy Special, *1994*

We purport to be very patriotic, but we somehow huckstered our national heritage. You know, it turns out that George Washington, especially for his time and his task, was a great man. He was tall, and imposing, and brave, and the right man at the right time, and risked being hung if we had lost the revolution. He was, in truth, the father of our country. And I'm sure that he'd be very, very thrilled to know that we sacredly observe his birthday each year with a mattress sale.

Robert Klein
Robert Klein on Broadway, *1986*

If you ever see me getting beaten by the police, put the video camera down and help me. Don't be chasing me around with a video camera. Don't be going, "I'll show this to Spike Lee in a few months." My hero during the riots was this guy—did anyone see the, uh, this guy ran out of a flaming building with a box of Pop Tarts? The Pop Tart bandit. I'm sure his parents were mighty proud.

Bobcat Goldthwait
The Best of Stand Up Spotlight, *1993*

Robert Klein

ROBERT KLEIN

Our TV went on in 1951 and has remained on practically ever since. There were so many television personalities who influenced my comedy: Lenny Bruce, Jonathan Winters, Jackie Gleason, Art Carney, Phil Silvers, Steve Allen, Red Buttons, Alan King, Don Rickles, Dick Shawn, Jack E. Leonard, Lucille Ball, Johnny Carson, Ernie Kovacs, Sid Caesar, and Groucho Marx are some of them, and I'm sure there are many more.

All of Phil Silvers's Sergeant Bilko *episodes were influential, mostly because of his energy, brashness, timing, and demeanor—not to mention Nat Hiken's wonderful cast of burlesque, vaudeville comedians and comedy character players.*

Other routines that were particularly influential include Sid Caeser's German professor, movie parodies, and mime bits; Steve Allen's various talk show stints (he was so innovative and quick, with lots of improvisation!); and Ernie Kovacs's Nairobi Trio and Percy Dovetonsils routines.

Alan King

MODERN ANGST

Angst, Comedy, and Bears

by Patricia Marx

"Of the world as it exists one cannot be enough afraid." Someone smart said this, I'm not sure who. But I'd like to add that one cannot be enough depressed, enough apprehensive, enough insecure, enough anguished, enough embarrassed, enough guilty, enough paranoid, enough hypochondriacal, enough in dread, enough in despair, or enough worried that the hum in this computer means that not just this file but everything I have written in the last three years is being destroyed, and since I have no copies of anything on disks I will never remember what I have written and so I will never be able to send out a résumé and I will have to find another career, which is impossible because I have no skills except nosing out parking spaces and forging the logo of Lord & Taylor, neither of which you can really call skills, or maybe the hum is the first sign of hearing loss and if you cannot hear then sooner or later you'll surely be hit by a bus. In short, one cannot have enough angst.

There are two kinds of angst, or anxiety, according to Freud—and he should know. *Realistic anxiety* is the rational, intelligible kind. Being nervous after a bear has just eaten your friend who was previously standing next to you is a good example. If you are too nervous to run, then your anxiety may be excessive and inexpedient, but it is not funny. *Neurotic anxiety*, which is unfounded, is the funnier kind of anxiety. Being nervous after a bear has just eaten your friend and then asking the waiter for the check is inapt. (Oh, God, do I mean inept?) Incidentally, there is also fretting, which is more congenial than anxiety. Fretting is what Bob Newhart does. If Bob Newhart's friend had just been eaten by a bear, he would nervously address the bear in order to get whatever information was needed to fill out the insurance forms.

Angst is not necessarily funny. Read Dostoyevsky. Or ask any psychiatrist how humorous his job is. Angst is particularly unfunny when it is happening to you. Certain people, though, are able to turn their woe into comic gold. Through invention, irony, and exaggeration, such people are able to expose their weaknesses and make us laugh instead of wince and want to send them off to an institution. "The loneliness of being left out, being thrown out, which I always fear and dread, is a great deal of my humor," says Joan Rivers. "My insecurity goes on and on and on," says Shelley Berman. "It's the most torturous thing in the world," he says. So, it makes sense that Berman calls his style "an attempt to entertain without inflicting pain."

The Bob Newhart Show
(1972–78)

You know me—I don't get no respect, no respect at all. The whole thing goes back to my childhood, the time I was lost on the beach and a cop helped me look for my parents. And I said to the cop, "Do you think we'll find them?" He said, "I don't know, kid, there's so many places they could hide."

Rodney Dangerfield
On Location with Rodney Dangerfield
1980

Nowadays you do what you're told—you don't argue with people—you get off where the cab driver lives. See this dress? I didn't want it, I was only looking. I said to the girl, "What's the size of the dress in the window?" She said, "It'll fit you." I said, "Well, what is it? A ten, a twelve?" She said, "It's your size, take it, that dress was made for you." I didn't even know I was gonna be in the neighborhood, she made a dress for me.

Jean Carroll
The Emerson Show: Toast of the Town
1949

Joan Rivers, Shelley Berman, Woody Allen, Richard Lewis, Rodney Dangerfield, and Garry Shandling. They are not a merry bunch. Rivers flits around the stage like a Pekingese on speed. Berman looks like he was just awakened from a nightmare. Allen is full of nervous tics. Lewis clutches at his hair and puts his hand to his forehead as if to take his temperature. Dangerfield strangles himself with his tie and sweats. Garry Shandling is the picture of someone in need of more antidepressants. This is not the group to invite, say, on a hayride. "I'm not a guy that characterizes anything as fun," says Garry Shandling. Richard Lewis notes that he has never answered, "Fine," to the question: "How are you?"

The world that these comedians occupy is bleak—"a bowl of pits," says Dangerfield. "It's very important to realize that we're up against an evil, insidious, hostile universe," writes Woody Allen in his play *Death*. "It'll make you ill and age you and kill you. And there's somebody—or something—out there who, for some irrational, unexplainable reason, is killing us." Shelley Berman told a reporter: "I, my wife, and my children are all living in the same dread, the same shadow of terror." His description of the dentist's waiting room might as well be the universe: "A few people seated around, huddled, each one an island unto himself. And you sit there, all by yourself, quietly suffering your own little personal chagrin because you know that everybody else in that room knows . . . that something in your mouth ain't right."

But Woody Allen, Shelley Berman, and the rest are not out to change the world, or even to satirize it, through laughter. Angst-driven comedy is too inward to be angry. Instead of lashing out at God, the government, or a romantic partner, these comics blame themselves and just mope. They expect the worst; they do not rebel against it. Reflecting on the human condition, Woody Allen does not take a stance of indignation. Rather, he wonders how he can believe in God when just last week he got his tongue caught in the roller of an electric typewriter. Garry Shandling casually mentions that he broke up with his girlfriend because she moved in with another guy. Shrugging, he adds, "And, hey, that's where I draw the line." There is nothing self-righteous about Richard Lewis, who explains that when he was on the high school debating team, instead of arguing, he would shout to the opposition, "I know you're right!"

If others are beyond criticism, the self is not. Rodney Dangerfield swears he hates himself so much that when girls tell him yes, he tells them to think it over. Joan Rivers can be hostile to certain celebrities—Liz Taylor, Princess Di, Madonna—but fundamentally, her humor comes from self-deprecation and self-doubt. Rivers mocks her breasts, her fat, her wrinkles. "They show my picture to men on death row to get their minds off women," she says. Before anyone can

Rodney Dangerfield

Woody Allen Looks at 1967 on *The Kraft Music Hall* (1967–71)

Joan Rivers

I was depressed for a long time. Nothing was going right for me. My analysis was not working out at all. My analyst didn't know what he was doing. He used to listen to my problems and write them down on a pad and then mail them in to Dear Abby.

Woody Allen
The Kraft Music Hall: *Woody Allen Looks At 1967*

You know, my mother calls, 5:30 in the morning. I'm sorry, I just, I don't get it. I'm not a dairy farmer, I don't like to get calls before six a.m. I have a theory, a crazy theory; I feel if the phone rings before six in the morning I automatically say "Death in the Family, Death in the Family."

Richard Lewis
I'm Exhausted, *1988*

jeer at or reject these comedians, they have done the job themselves—and much more thoroughly than their imagined adversaries ever could.

Whatever happens, it is always bad. You win the lottery—you have reduced your chances for winning again. You are granted immortality—you'll have to get another battery for your lifetime-guaranteed wristwatch. Even the glimmer of hope is unthinkable. Discussing how traumatic it was to be fired from Fox, Joan Rivers confides to Alan King, "No matter how good my career gets again, I will always know in my heart that it is not something I thought it was. I wish I could have dreams. Fantasies. No more. I never will. That's gone." Garry Shandling believes his career is a fluke. "Things are going well, but my blood type is still very negative," says Richard Lewis on *Late Night* when David Letterman comments about Lewis's recent professional success. Woody Allen used to cover his ears to

Fortunately my parents were intelligent, enlightened people. They accepted me exactly for what I was—a punishment from God.

David Steinberg
The Flip Wilson Show, *1971*

Richard Lewis
Opposite:
Garry Shandling

Shelley Berman

SHELLEY BERMAN

The Ed Sullivan Show, *for all its fine exposure and good money, could sometimes be a comedian's hell. On more than one occasion closing credits could be seen rolling over a comic's act. It was well known that on this show you came in on time or else. Generally, you had no more than five or six minutes to create and sustain hilarity. Yet, Sullivan was perhaps the greatest showman since P. T. Barnum.*

As a frequent guest comedian on The Ed Sullivan Show, *I knew the rules. You did your spot twice on the Sunday shooting. Both shows were taped. If you ran over your allotted time, you could count on Ed calling you into his office between tapings. He'd ask you to cut. Even more galling, he was brilliant enough to know just what you should* cut.

On one memorable shot, I did a routine called "Father and Son." It was a funny, biographical routine which took on a poignant turn in the latter half. It ran a full twelve minutes in the afternoon shoot.

My call came and I went down to his office prepared for the worst. He greeted me somberly and muttered something about nice work. Then he said, "You know the part where you tell your son to write a letter? Well, let me make a suggestion. Add a line to that, saying something like, 'Write the letter to your mother.'" Add?

I did what he said, adding time to the spot. As I performed, I became aware of a lighting transition, significantly enhancing the work. Violin music came in, emphasizing the bittersweet ending. The routine earned a powerful reception. And when I came off stage, Sullivan's wife was waiting on the phone to congratulate me.

A dentist's waiting room is a smartly furnished chamber of horrors. Well, isn't it? You know, with the cracked leather furniture and the one coat rack? And it's covered with coats and there's nobody in the waiting room, you know . . . you wonder where they went. Or maybe there are a few people seated about, huddled, each one an island unto himself. And you sit there all by yourself, quietly suffering your own little personal chagrin because you know that everybody else *in the room knows that something in your mouth* ain't *right.*

Shelley Berman
The Ed Sullivan Show, *1962*

block out the applause following his stand-up. "I'd like to leave you with something positive," he once said as he left the stage. "But I can't think of anything positive to say. Would you take two negatives?"

What is wrong with these people? Why are they so miserable? Everytime I try to come up with a pattern of explanation, it falls apart. Height? Woody Allen is short, the rest are all more or less average. Place of birth? They were all born in New York, except Shelley Berman and Garry Shandling, who were born in Chicago. (Garry Shandling moved to Arizona when he was three and Richard Lewis was "lowered" in New Jersey.) Hair? All the men are balding, except Richard Lewis and Garry Shandling, who are nevertheless obsessed with their hair. None of them drives a Chevy Impala, but this does not elucidate anything.

Perhaps we can blame their parents. They do—both in their acts and in their lives. Woody Allen jokes, "When I was kidnapped, my parents snapped into action. They rented out my room." Rodney Dangerfield carps that his mother never breast-fed him. "She told me she liked me as a friend," he says. Richard

Lewis describes his mother as someone so neurotic she sent mixed messages to the dog—"Fetch. See if I care."

Upon examination, however, all of these angst-ridden comedians had okay-enough childhoods, with the exception of Garry Shandling, whose thirteen-year-old brother died when Garry was ten. Woody Allen's parents quarreled and he regrets he didn't grow up in Manhattan; Shelley Berman felt his father was hard to communicate with; Rodney Dangerfield was poor; Richard Lewis's caterer father was rarely home; Joan Rivers's doctor father could never make enough money to satisfy her mother. These charges are insufficient cause for such profound angst.

And so, I turn again to Freud. Freud believed that frustration of the sex drive triggers anxiety. If you know anything about Freud, you know that he drags sex into everything. This is not to say that the subject of sex and its scarcity doesn't recur in stand-up routines. "I once made love for an hour and fifteen minutes. It was on the day you push the clocks ahead," says Garry Shandling. Joan Rivers bemoans that it's been so long since she's had sex, she can't even remember who gets tied up. Rodney Dangerfield complains that if it weren't for pickpockets, he'd have no sex life at all. Somehow, though, the problem of sex seems symptomatic, rather than primal. These comedians look as if they were born with mid-life crises.

Which brings us to Freud's more interesting, or at least wackier, theory. Angst, he suggests, is approximately our first sensation. It is what we feel during birth, an experience so horrific and painful that those unpleasurable physiological feelings, combined with the panic associated with separation from the mother, are repeated through our lives as the state of anxiety. In fact, as Freud points out, the word angst is from the same root as the Latin and German words "angustiae" and "enge," meaning "narrow place or straits"—as in birth canal. You are probably thinking: Okay, but what if your mother had a Caesarian section? The ever clever Freud has wriggled a way out. Even if you did not personally experience the act of birth, he declares, the state of anxiety has been so fully ingrained into the species that you will *never ever escape.*

While this may give us another reason to blame our mothers, it does not really explain why Woody Allen, Shelley Berman, Rodney Dangerfield, Richard Lewis, Joan Rivers, and Garry Shandling are so funny.

We laugh until we hurt—they hurt until we laugh.

My luck is so bad I can't do nothing right. Opened my fortune cookie and there was a summons. Bought my wife one of these new water beds; come home four o'clock in the morning, there's a guy in the middle of the floor. I said, "Who's that?" She said, "Lifeguard." My luck is terrible—I called suicide prevention; they put me on hold.

Slappy White
The Flip Wilson Show, *1972*

Now I got a new thing; this is the new thing, Tom. It's called Jewish boxing—you don't hit the guy; you just make him feel guilty.

Billy Crystal as Muhammad Ali to Harry Shearer as Tom Snyder
The T.V. Show, *1979*

I'm not sure how many of you out here—and there—are concerned with how you spend your leisure time. Obviously this is a careless group; you're watching television when you could be doing something constructive, like putting your spice rack in order alphabetically. I mean truthfully, how many of us are as comfortable with the rosette attachment on our icing gun as we'd like to be? Not many, I dare say.

Lily Tomlin
Lily, *1973*

The Tonight Show . . .
and Other Political Platforms

by Tony Hendra

"I like fun, but we don't have time for jokes. We have to overthrow our government." Thus spake Mort Sahl, the father of modern political humor, at the Democratic convention in Los Angeles in 1960. Innocuous though Sahl's pseudo-subversion may sound now, it gave Eisenhower-era America hot flashes. It had only been a few years since Senator McCarthy's Communist-style purge of the Communists under every American bed; and the McCarthy-inspired Communist Control Act of 1954 was still in force, clearly stating that communism advocated "the violent overthrow of government."

Sahl was no Communist. But he was the leader of a new, edgy, aggressive, unapologetically smart brand of satirical commentary that questioned every social and political assumption of postwar society. Together with his fierce rival, Lenny Bruce, Sahl had already overthrown if not the government, the domesticated ethnicity of radio-era comedy. In so doing he altered the course of American humor. Woody Allen once said of Sahl, "Without him there wouldn't have been (modern humor). He made the country receptive to a kind of comedy it was not used to hearing." Yet Sahl and Bruce brought about this sea change with almost no help from television.

In the highly charged, black-and-white (or perhaps Red-and-white) political atmosphere of the late fifties it was understandable that network executives might mistake the new humor for Communist humor. Throughout the fifties all three networks had Standards and Practices departments with a panoply of rules about what could and couldn't be said on the air; to these were added unwritten rules about taboo subjects: religion, narcotics, sex, the military, nuclear terror, censorship itself. So a double standard arose, even as a new generation of Sahl-and-Bruce-inspired comedians like Dick Gregory, Lily Tomlin, George Carlin, Godfrey Cambridge, Richard Pryor, and a constant stream of Second City graduates (Shelley Berman and David Steinberg, for example) were emerging to explore just such subjects. The new comedians, who daily inhaled the heady politics of the sixties, understood that while they were relatively free to say what they pleased on the folk/jazz club/college concert circuit, they had to check their First Amendment rights at the studio door.

Yet television wasn't an entirely monolithic opponent. The same year Congress passed the Communist Control Act, 1954, NBC put young comic/musician Steve Allen into its 11:30 P.M. slot nationally and created what would become the

The Tonight Show Starring Johnny Carson

Mort Sahl

As you know there's been a lot of talk about the U2 in the last couple of weeks. That started on the first of May when the plane was shot down and the president reserved comment until he could assemble all the facts, weigh them, and discuss it with his advisers—and then deny it. And so Khrushchev turned around and said, "I'm sure the president didn't know about the flight," and the State Department said, "Of course he knew," and the president said, "Yes, I've known about all the flights." So then the plane was shot down, although it was 13,000 miles inside Russia and we weren't sure how [they saw it] unless they looked down and spotted it. And the president said, "Why are they so self-righteous, they've got a lot of spies in our country too"—which they have, and if we're lucky they may steal some of our secrets and then they'll be two years behind.

Mort Sahl
The Steve Allen Plymouth Show, *1960*

prime locus of mainstream political humor for decades—*The Tonight Show.* *
Throughout the fifties Allen sought out nonconformist guests like Sahl and Bruce.
Tamed and tempered though their material had to be, Allen's respect for them
helped to ratify the new wave. His *Tonight Show* replacement, Jack Paar, went further, fighting battles with network censors, adopting political causes, and present-

* *Editor's Note: The formal title of this program has changed over time: among other permutations it has
been called* Tonight, *with Steve Allen as host (September 27, 1954–January 25, 1957);* The Jack Paar
Show *(July 29, 1957–March 30, 1962);* The Tonight Show Starring Johnny Carson *(October 1, 1962–
May 22, 1992); and* The Tonight Show with Jay Leno *(May 25, 1992–present). For the section on political humor we will use* The Tonight Show *throughout.*

Pat Paulsen for President, the prime-time "campaign" special (1968)

Dan Rowan: I don't care what your politics are, you don't call the president of the United States Old Dick. He's the president.

Dick Martin: We've known him for twenty years.

Rowan: I don't care how long we've known him, you don't call the president Old Dick.

Martin: He was a regular on our show.

Rowan: That doesn't make any difference. When you talk to him it's Mr. President.

Martin: How about Mr. Dick?

Rowan: Mr.—from the minute a man is elected to that office he is called Mr. President. His most intimate friends, Mr. President. Never anything else. From the day he's elected till the day he dies. If Harry Truman takes a walk around the block, "Good morning, Mr. President." Same thing with Johnson: "Good morning, Mr. President."

Martin: Hmmm. Late at night, upstairs?

Rowan: Well, I don't know—I suppose Mrs. Nixon calls him whatever she used to call him, I don't know.

Martin: Tricky Dick!

Dan Rowan and Dick Martin
The Tonight Show Starring Johnny Carson: 10th Anniversary, 1972

ing a long parade of brilliant young comedians, including Nichols and May, Jonathan Winters, and in the first Kennedy year, when lunch counters and civil rights were *the* issue, Dick Gregory. After one appearance on Paar, Gregory neatly expressed the irony of performing ultra-political material to a nation still unconvinced that civil rights wasn't a commie plot: "If you actually like me, you'll invite me to lunch when it *isn't* Brotherhood Week." Burnt out by 1962, Paar gave way to Johnny Carson, who quickly made *The Tonight Show* his own institution, and his monologue a nightly must-see of topical commentary.

The political satire that flourished on and off TV during the Kennedy years was chilled to the bone by his assassination. Reflecting the trend during the run up to the 1964 presidential election, NBC repeatedly preempted the American version of *That Was the Week That Was*, which included satirical luminaries like Buck Henry and writer Herb Sargent; the next year *TW3* was canceled.

One school of thought holds that political humor *needs* censorship, thrives on it. The late fifties and sixties may well have produced such giants of humor precisely because they had to fight for their material, sharpening their wits on the whetstone of repression. To be sure the games that were played with censors on *The Smothers Brothers Comedy Hour* produced some of its funniest stuff. Pat Paulsen's 1968 yearlong run for the presidency was a satirical achievement unequaled before or since, and it spun off countless gems: "I want to entertain the troops," said the candidate piously at one point, ". . . in Chicago." CBS Program Practices rode the campaign material relentlessly, but producer Tommy Smothers eluded them at every turn. (Smothers would have Paulsen fidget around when taping a piece, which not only gave the candidate his trademark shiftiness, but made him impossible to edit in those technically more primitive days.) Similar games were played on NBC's *Laugh-In*, which had zoomed to Number 1 in the Nielsens, to a large degree on the strength of its political content. The two shows, on rival networks, shared a generational and political bond. The *New York Times* took this common humor very seriously, seeing it as a cure for TV's "isolation from the realities of the surrounding world"—code for Vietnam. TV correspondent Jack Gould wrote in 1968: "The sacred cows of today's society are no longer immune to the irreverence of the newer school of comedians . . . (Rowan and Martin and the Smothers Brothers) may be the instrument for gradually and subtly bringing TV into the mainstream of modern concern."

Alas, not quite. The fragile physique of political humor turned out to be no match for the "realities of the surrounding world." The media were squarely blamed for the chaotic violence at the Democratic convention in Chicago; to oldline Democrats it was radical firebrands like the Smothers who had incited the kids to riot and helped to paint the picture of a party ripped to shreds by the war. Time to talk network regulation. In the 1968 fall season, despite great ratings, CBS began distancing itself from the Smothers, chopping holes in the show almost every week. On Good Friday, 1969, the Brothers were dumped.

In terms of visibility and controversy the 1968 election was a high point for cutting-edge political satire on television. Its effectiveness was quite another matter. This was only the third presidential election in which TV had been a major factor. As live performers who'd cut their teeth in clubs and concerts, the Smothers Brothers could be forgiven for thinking of it as an electronic extension of a night-club stage, but with a vastly larger audience. Their experience showed that television had become much more than that: it had become a parallel reality with its own rules, where it wasn't enough to be right, or even hilarious; where your performance was always open to unforeseen interpretation by TV's rules. In the Smothers case, their satire wasn't part of the solution, but part of the problem. This principle is as relevant today as it was then. Political humor on television is inseparable from the effect television has on politics.

Stand-up political comedy entered a long media twilight after this. Satirical energy migrated to sitcoms, like *M*A*S*H, All in the Family,* and *The Mary Tyler Moore Show.* Two of the more successful comedians of the sixties, Pryor and Carlin, went through radical transformations around 1970, both emerging as major artists, but their new plans didn't include television. (No better evidence for this exists than Carlin's classic 1972 routine: "Seven Words You Can Never Say on Television.") One light in the gloom was *The Tonight Show*—the only successful comedy show in the early seventies where you got topical humor with any bite. While Carson's monologue had not become the national political bellwether that it was in the Reagan years, it already reflected the country's political mood. Anti-Kissinger material evidenced a shift in the nation's sentiments toward the war; once anti-Nixon jokes became a staple during Watergate, the president's days were numbered. It's worth noting that network censors had always given Carson more leeway in his political references (and sexual innuendo) than they did to younger performers—the flip side of that old double standard. *The Tonight Show* was ultra-acceptable to NBC—providing in some years 15–20 percent of the network's entire profits—and Carson was reliably Over Thirty (he was forty-four in the watershed year 1970). Which demonstrates another enduring principle of political humor on television—you can't say anything dangerous until you've been proven safe.

And that raises the question: what's the purpose of political humor on television anyhow? The Smothers undoubtedly wanted their humor to affect policy.

I had a meeting with the entire membership of the Amalgamated Consolidated Negro Republicans—three of the nicest guys you'd ever want to meet. And we joined forces with the New Black Democrats, and the five of us went over, we went over and we challenged the joint session of Congress on minority inclusion. We asked them straightforward: "Is there hope?" We said, "Can a Negro ever become President?" They said, "Yes, if he runs against a Puerto Rican."

Nipsey Russell
The Jackie Gleason Show, *1969*

More allegations about Supreme Court judge Clarence Thomas. A new book called **Capital Games** *alleges that while at Yale, Thomas used to frequent theaters that showed double X, triple X, and quadruple X films. . . . You know what I like about Judge Thomas? He always has a way of taking a negative situation like this and turning it into something positive. He claims that the only reason he went to see those X films is because he thought they were documentaries about Malcolm.*

Arsenio Hall
The Arsenio Hall Show, *1992*

BILL MAHER

One comedian who's had a great influence on me is Dean Martin. Everyone knows the groundbreaking work that Dean and Jerry Lewis did in their early days together, but even though the duo literally changed the face of comedy, few acknowledge Dean's enormous contribution and prodigious talent. When the history of comedy is written by someone who really knows the subject, he or she will have to give Dean his rightful due.

I suppose Dean has been overlooked because he was a gifted singer and suave ladies' man. His timing was impeccable, and he had to be the smoothest straight man ever to play the game. Even now, I still wish I could be that silver-tongued, tuxedo-wearing Italian crooner. Legend has it that Dean only came to the office one day a week, and even then he was drunk. That's a track record I still shoot for. Despite contractual obligations that stipulate otherwise, I show up drunk three days a week, and wish I could get it down to just one.

Carson, a heartland moderate (as far as anyone could tell) wasn't that presumptuous. Laughs were what he was after; the more people agree with the thrust of a political joke, the bigger the laugh. The irony was that the Smothers's confrontational attempts to change people's minds probably had less effect on policy than Carson's cooler *vox populi* approach. His monologue might mostly entertain, but every now and then it could unearth some hitherto submerged consensus. In a democracy simple affirmation of public sentiment can have far-reaching consequences. There's no poll as conclusive as a huge laugh.

As the stand-up renaissance of the seventies got under way, Carson became more and more influential, not just as a showcaser of new talent, but as the dominant voice of political humor. He didn't have a lot of competition. For all its revolutionary reputation, the original cast of *SNL* wasn't that interested in politics. (Writer and script consultant Herb Sargent noted that few of the cast or staff ever bothered to vote at election time.) *SNL* certainly gave many of its comedic hosts a freer platform than they'd been used to, and Chevy Chase's rubbery lampoon of President Ford may have contributed to his election defeat. But even the officially topical "Weekend Update" tended to emphasize *SNL's* trademark, character formation rather than politics. *SNL,* in fact, was on the cusp of a backlash against the intense politicization of the previous two decades; even as comedy outlets like HBO and comedians of all shapes and sizes multiplied in the late seventies, politics became too obvious, and old-fashioned, a subject. Mark Russell's PBS specials from Buffalo stood out in this environment, but blistering though they could be, they were regarded as Kennedy-era throwbacks by the newly media-hip

Politically Incorrect (debuted in 1993) panel with Sam Donaldson, Rep. Bob Dornan, host Bill Maher, Harriett Woods, and Al Franken

The Robert Mapplethorpe exhibit was closed down. Now, Mapplethorpe's a dead gay artist and he can still piss off Jesse Helms, so, he's a hero in my book.

Bobcat Goldthwait
The Best of Stand Up Spotlight, *1993*

ex-underground and not-so-nonconformists. At the end of the day in the brick-wall comedy clubs the action was elsewhere—childhood, lifestyle trivia, sex, drugs, and above all TV itself.

In 1982 Letterman gave this new, entrepreneurial, politically disengaged comedy a permanent home, and made it the dominant form of the eighties. But as cracks appeared in Reagan's city on the hill, politics began edging its way back into stand-up—notably in the person of political impressionist Jim Morris, whose brilliantly crafted Reagan first appeared in the mid-eighties. Morris stood out from his apolitical peers, not least from the latex-freak impressionists of *SNL*. Great Survivor George Carlin regularly included inspired political rants in his HBO specials, for example, in his attack on the more than three hundred indicted members of the Reagan administration: "These were the folks who got elected on the issue of law and order. . . they're against street crime so long as it isn't Wall Street."

As the city on the hill melted away altogether, political one-liners began to crop up in everyone's act. But times had changed in the twenty years since political humor was last in vogue. The lack of censorship in the stand-up's venue of choice, cable TV, meant that practically anything could be said. This was ideal in theory, but in practice, when anything can be said, little sticks. There were those who'd paid their satirical dues back when it wasn't so cool to be political—Richard Belzer, Will Durst, George Wallace—but they tended to get lost in the crush of mediocre, interchangeable issue-zingers.

Furthermore, television had by now completely subsumed politics, requiring political figures to perform, however ineptly, like any other television personalities. The Smothers Principle applied—political humor on television is inseparable from the effect television has on politics. Once television reduces politics to a form of entertainment, political humor becomes little more than dramatic criticism—entertainers assessing other entertainers. Thus, Bobcat Goldthwait reacting to the Iran-Contra hearings, dealt with Ollie North's "amazing acting" by observing that, "it was like Jimmy Stewart in *It's a Wonderful Life*. I mean I wanted to get the guy but after five minutes I'm going: 'You know he's got some valid points.'"

Other than Jay Leno, who gets too little credit for continuing Carson's grand tradition in his *Tonight Show* monologue, two people in particular have cut themselves out from the pack. One is Dennis Miller, who finally brought teeth to "Weekend Update" when he hit *SNL* and continues to infuse his material with intelligence and perspective; for example, his comment that opposing the Russian sale of nuclear technology to Iran was shortsighted given that they were responsible for Chernobyl. The other is Bill Maher, whose *Politically Incorrect* gets the same smart, edgy result from throwing political figures together with comedians. Both

Dennis Miller

Reagan's getting up there, huh? Seventy-seven at the end of this next term. Seventy-seven and he has access to the button. You know, my grandfather is seventy-seven—we don't let him use the remote control for the TV set.

Dennis Miller
It's Showtime at the Apollo!, *1987*

Miller and Maher push themselves to break out of the incestuous TV-about-TV trap of most current humor; they deal with real world events and do their home-work about the issues. In this respect they approach the status of news analysts, except they're far more memorable than the pundit parade. As journalism becomes more like entertainment, entertainers like Maher and Miller are becoming more like journalists. It seems probable that the process will go one step further, as it does occasionally on Don Imus's radio show—a total fusion of news and comedy. When it does, it will inject a fierce new focus and energy to political humor on television. And it will close a circle, harking back more than thirty years to one of the earliest and purest forms of political humor on TV—*That Was the Week That Was*—which, first and foremost, was a news program.

Which brings us back to Mort Sahl. As he is fond of saying, true to his form onstage rather than on television: "I guess this means Darwin was wrong."

A Funny Thing Happened on the Way to the White House

by Marvin Kitman

The founding father of stand-up political comedy for me was Bob Hope. Old Ski Nose, as we used to call him, made fun of presidents starting with George Washington, all of whom he knew intimately. He even may have played golf with George III in Scotland. The good stand-up political comedian, as Bob and Ray defined him, was "nondenominational" in party politics, and Hope in his early years was fearless, deflating our leaders regardless of party affiliation with one-liners and zingers.

And then there were his famous Christmas show specials. I grew up thinking that the purpose of wars was to provide Bob Hope with TV specials. I used to love to see him swinging his golf club surrounded by the boys in a hangar or staggering onto the decks of aircraft carriers in one of those silly admiral caps. Hope was nobody's fool. You take guys in combat eleven months, fired at by Japanese, Germans, Vietcong, Arabs, Bulgarians, or Freedonians—it didn't matter—they tended to be rather enthusiastic. Especially when Hope was accompanied by somebody like Rita Hayworth or the bevy of Hopeful starlets. Hope wasn't stupid. This way the USO picked up expenses for production costs. And he had a built-in laugh track.

The next thing I knew, especially when he started becoming a confidant of Dwight Eisenhower, Hope was *vieux chapeau*. Maybe he played golf with Ike once too often. Somehow he became too much an insider, and for us sophisticates he was as funny about politics as your average cabinet secretary in the first Nixon-Agnew administration. That's how I knew I was in my Mort Sahl period. I still remember how excited I was the first time I saw Mort Sahl on TV, with his rolled newspaper, giving his "State of the Nation" address.

Mort Sahl was the love child of Will Rogers, whom I always thought of as the first political stand-up comedian. Rogers would have been very big on TV, if he hadn't listened to Wiley Post and his silly trip idea in 1935. He was a very visual stand-up comic, who did stupid rope tricks onstage, the movies, and radio while commenting on the news of the day.

Will Rogers's material came from the newspapers. "All I know," he used to say, "is just what I read in the papers." His act, he explained about his secret formula, was buying the morning papers and just recounting what happened the previous day in Congress.

Of course he had a lot to work with at that time. Cal Coolidge was a funny guy. And don't forget Herbert Hoover. His jokes—"a chicken in every pot"

Tom and Dick Smothers on
The Smothers Brothers Comedy Hour

Bob Hope visits a military base at
Christmas

BOB HOPE

*We were taping on the flight deck of an aircraft carrier during one of the overseas
shows for the GIs when the wind caught all the cue cards and threw them to the deck.
What could I say but, "Wait a minute . . . there go all my ad-libs."*

*How about that election. California's back
to a two party system . . . the Democrats
and the Screen Actors Guild. It's the biggest
victory for an actor since Charlton Heston
parted the Red Sea. When Ronny heard he
was elected governor he was thrilled. He
said, "Good. Now when do I get the script?"*

Bob Hope
Chrysler Presents: A Bob Hope Comedy
Special, *1966*

and "prosperity is just around the corner"—kept them in stitches during the
Depression.

But, it was not topical humor as much as commentary that Will Rogers pioneered, a tradition that Mort Sahl carried on. Sahl actually carried a newspaper
rolled in his hand all the time. Was it the same one, I used to wonder, watching
him on TV, or did he change it every day?

"I sat with Mort Sahl in Mr. Kelly's, an old jazz club in Chicago gone now,
back in the seventies," recalled Roger Ailes, a TV producer then who went on to
become a political consultant to presidents and is now president of a TV network
(CNBC), "and watched him read a paper in a booth. He got up onstage six hours
later that night with forty minutes of new material. With no writers. He just did
what he had seen in the afternoon papers. He was a genius."

I am still wowed by that story, especially in this day when I keep reading in
the papers that *Saturday Night Live* is dying because they have too many writers
who can't get laughs, and nobody can understand why.

Mort Sahl made a name for himself, such as it was, in the McCarthy Era.
The fifties were a period of repression and fear, and when Mort spoke out we were
thrilled as well as entertained. At last somebody told the truth, in contrast to all
the lies in the media. His act, whenever it got on to TV, was the place where Adlai
Stevenson had a chance. His Joe McCarthy, Ike, Nixon, Checkers, Sherman Adams,
and vicuña coat jokes were the sort of stuff that you would talk about at the water
cooler the next day, and I would have, too, if I could only have found a job.

The big thing for the last thirty-two years of Mort's act has been the Kennedy
assassination. His obsession with who killed JFK was the death of him. Just as
Lenny Bruce became obsessed with his prosecution and the court system. They
both became preachers.

Stand-up political comedy based on news and information had a golden
age on *The Smothers Brothers Comedy Hour,* a variety show on CBS, which I used
to watch religiously from 1967 to 1969. Tom and Dick touched a chord, or an
exposed nerve, in the TV audience. It wasn't just young people, the so-called
counterculture. There was a growing disenchantment with what TV viewers were

Bob Hope

Dick Smothers: *We lost another airplane —crashed in Greenland—and we lost four hydrogen bombs in the Arctic snow. That's disturbing to me. Very. Seriously.*

Tom Smothers: *Not to me.*

Dick: *What do you mean?*

Tom: *Well, I think that just simply reflects another change in the hydrogen bomb policy. I mean, we're losing them in the snow in Greenland now instead of the waters of Spain like we used to. I think that's it. I feel like it's a step in the right direction in order to spread democracy.*

Dick: *Spread democracy?*

Tom: *Yeah.*

Dick: *Don't you realize that losing hydrogen bombs disturbs all the . . . nuclear powers who control world politics?*

Tom: *Maybe they need to be disturbed.*

Dick: *Here are the powers that control world politics, that have the bomb, right? The U. S., right? Russia, Red China, England, and France.*

Tom: *Yeah, but now they've added two fishermen in Spain and three Eskimos in Greenland.*

Tom and Dick Smothers
The Smothers Brothers Comedy Hour
1968

Congressional majority—*this is a horrible story, I was reading it—uh, congressional majority leader Dick Armey—that's his real name, he's the congressional majority leader—he called gay congressman Barney Frank, Barney Fag. Now I just want to say this, uh, to Dick Armey: If there's one thing you can say for Dick, at least you don't have to mispronounce his name to say what you think about him.*

Jon Stewart
The Jon Stewart Show, *1995*

reading in the papers and especially seeing on TV news in the "living room war," a disillusionment with American foreign policy. They were mad at the government for where it was going in Vietnam. Unfortunately, the excuses, the glowing reports of success and being able to see the light at the end of the tunnel, didn't wash. Uncle Walter Cronkite was telling us "And that's the way it is," reciting the Pentagon line. But elsewhere on CBS, Tom and Dick and their counterculture stand-up comic guests were saying: hold on, this is the way it really is.

The Smothers Brothers were the Palace of political comedy acts, giving a platform to the new young comics like George Carlin. It was they who brought Jackie Mason back from exile, after he had given Ed Sullivan the wrong finger. On January 19, 1969, his first appearance on the Smothers show, Mason gave the best single performance of political stand-up comedy I had ever seen. It was nine incredible minutes, with Jackie giving a sermon on the need for brotherhood and tolerance for everybody regardless of race, creed, or color. "But not you, mister. You I don't like." While calling on all Americans to support the new president (Nixon), he explained the Vietnam War ("Are you listening, mister?"), and reported that we were blowing up five hundred bridges a week. "I'm just back from Vietnam," he told the audience. "They only have eight bridges in the whole country." Jackie gave a military secret: "What we do is drop the bridges first. Then we blow them up." It was brilliant, the way to make political stand-up comedy go down in skittish times, when the network was having kittens at the mention of Vietnam.

The Smothers had one good thing going for them in terms of political comedy: opposition. Somebody was out to censor them, the good guys. The bad guys, the black hats, the network, the establishment, the thought police were on their case. That made every performance exciting. When you laughed at a joke about the absurdity of Vietnam you were scoring a point. It was not couch potato TV.

And then the word finally came down from Black Rock. As it was described to me by one veteran network executive, CBS had only two options: "1) Either fire them, or 2) send them to Vietnam." The network opted for the softer penalty and just fired them.

There was risk in political comedy in the old days. You put your career in jeopardy if you got out there too far. There was something subversive about poking fun at the establishment. You weren't just shooting arrows in the air. The targets got upset. They would bleed when hit.

Stand-up political comedy on TV went into a coma during the Reagan years, a period described in the British TV stand-up puppet show *Spitting Image*'s hilarious 1984 series of sketches called "The President's Brain Is Missing." Politics as a subject for young comics was replaced by drugs and sex. On cable and in the

Jackie Mason

clubs, it was the age of schmutz comedy. All you had to do to get a laugh was to say one of the seven dirty words you weren't allowed to use on the networks, as George Carlin explained on public radio one night, starting a federal case.

Johnny Carson kept the genre of the political roast alive. His *Tonight Show* was the only place you could hear the humor of dissent on the networks. It has been said that if it weren't for stand-up political comedians in the Berlin cabarets in the thirties, Hitler would have risen to power. But Carson was truly a force to reckon with in terms of impact. When Carson started getting laughs with Nixon-as-a-crook jokes, it was a turning point for the president, a bad moment,

Mark Russell

In Congress they actually are voting, voting mind you, about whether or not to grant a formal apology to the Japanese-Americans who were interned in detention camps at the end of World War II, forty-six years ago. You know, if I was one of the survivors, I would tell them to take their apology and shove it up their caucus. . . . Now I read where the president may veto the apology. Well, that's understandable, I mean after all in World War II it was a Japanese-American actor who shot Reagan down . . . in the movie Hellcats of the Navy.

Mark Russell
Mark Russell Comedy Special, *1987*

MARK RUSSELL

If you can reach your sixties and still have a mentor, Mort Sahl is mine. He first taught me that conservatives make great targets and I thought, "Hey, this is easy." But he then moved on to the second lesson: don't leave out the liberals, so you can find out who your friends are. Mort Sahl is a moralist without an 800-number and a monologuist whose dinner table conversations could be published without editing.

yet another crisis in a life of crises. If Carson got a laugh, politicians had to worry. He was a barometer of public opinion, reflecting what the country was thinking.

Why did Johnny have such impact? First of all, you've got to remember it was the early seventies. In New York City, cable TV existed only in Manhattan, where people couldn't get reception. The only thing on cable TV was Robin Byrd. Carson was America's foreplay. Besides, he was very funny.

He had a neat hard edge to his political comedy. He could get away with it because he was so unthreatening. He was a corn-fed American midwesterner with an innocent face and good posture, not some bearded Trotskyite Bolshevik deviationist beast.

And he could do extremely biting jokes. In 1989, a big issue in the papers was Bush wanting to veto the minimum wage bill in order "to look tough." "Why does he have to look tough?" asked Johnny one night. "Why doesn't he look tough against Exxon?" It got "few laughs, but lots of applause," *Time* magazine reported at the time. And it drew blood. Take Alexander Haig, for example. Johnny ruined Haig's life after he announced that 'I'm in charge here,' while President Reagan was asleep or was in the hospital. It was tough for any public official to recapture his dignity after Carson.

The big difference in political stand-up comedy today is that it is more surface, lacking in cogent point of view, the very antithesis of Mort Sahl, and this may be a reflection more of the audience than comedians. To get Mort Sahl's humor you had to read a newspaper. Two papers would help even more. Today all you have to do is watch the TV tabloid magazines. The jokes are not about news or information but gossip. The latest president's girlfriend or the O. J. trial. Take the latest gossip and give it a twist, and it's heavy political comedy.

The truth is that all you have to do to get a laugh today is mention a name: "Newt Gingrich" is like "Brooklyn" used to be, or Jack Benny saying, "Anaheim, Azusa, and Cucamonga." A perfect example of name-dropping is what David Letterman did at the 1995 Oscars. He was bombing with his opening monologue.

He knew that if he said "Newt Gingrich" he would get a big laugh with the Holly-wood crowd. It wasn't even a joke. He just suddenly threw out the notion of Newt Gingrich working at Blockbuster. What kind of joke was that? But it got him back on track. That's the way it works today.

How about the new breed of political stand-up comics? Dennis Miller is very good, more literate than others. He reads newspapers, like Mort Sahl. He's smart. And that's why he'll never be a huge success. He's over people's heads. The average TV viewer, it's said, has a twelve-year-old mentality; Miller is for the fourteen-year-olds. He also comes across as a smart ass, who only appeals to other smart asses in the audience.

Whenever I despair about the decline of stand-up political comedy, and west-ern civilization, whichever is more important, I like to listen to my Mark Russell tapes. It renews my faith to hear those immortal words "Live from Buffalo" on "federally funded public TV," as he calls it in homage to Newt. Mark Russell, the Beltway comic, who, since 1975, has been going to Buffalo to do a series of specials on public TV station WNED, is a musical Mort Sahl. He is Will Rogers playing a piano and telling jokes based not only on reading the newspapers. In his 1990 year-end special, he actually read verbatim from the budget for fiscal 1991 and got big laughs. He explained the theoretical underpinning of the Bush administration closing military bases: "They had finally learned Bunker Hill, Appomatox, and Fort Sumter have lost their usefulness." The two criteria for closing bases, Russell explained: "a) outmoded; b) located in home districts of a Democratic congress-man." He made jokes about our Social Security taxes going into El Salvador death squads, the peace dividend from the end of the Vietnam war having gone into infrastructure (a bank in Switzerland).

I especially love to hear his patter songs. Who else would stand up at a piano and sing a song about the killing of beloved Romanian Premier Nicolae Ceausescu, who was so beloved the people wanted to kill him even after he was executed, which he did to the tune of "Chattanooga Choo Choo": "Pardon me boys, are you the cats who shot Ceausescu?"

C-SPAN proves Will Rogers's theory best. All you have to do is turn it on and watch Congress and the Senate doing their thing. C-SPAN has replaced my favorite humor magazine, the *Congressional Record*, as a source of stand-up political comedy.

During the debate Ross Perot said that because of his stance on NAFTA, six Cuban assassins had been hired to kill him. He was outraged, he was angry, he said, "Those are jobs that should have gone to Americans."

David Letterman
Late Show with David Letterman, *1993*

THE OBSERVATIONALIST

So What's the Deal With . . .?

by Douglas Coupland

What's the deal with premoistened towelettes?

We all know them. They're small ... they're premoistened ... they smell like lemon tetrachloride ... they come in small foil wrappers that dream only of choking the local landfill ... flight attendants hurl them at you on commuter air flights ... and no franchised chicken dinner could possibly be complete without one. And so the question remains: what's the deal with premoistened towelettes?

Exactly.

Anybody can describe a premoistened towelette to you, but it takes a good observational comedian to tell you what, exactly, is the deal with them. Such is the nature of observational comedy. Observational comedy doesn't depend on situation or character or anything but a lone noble comedian adrift in the modern world, observing the unobservable—those banalities and fragments of minutiae lurking just below the threshold of perception: cineplex candy; remote control units; Topsy Tails; Florida; Cycle Three dog food; tabloid romances; and Whaler fish-filet-type sandwiches. So what we're discussing here is actually, what's the deal with what's-the-deal?

Pop artists may have shocked a culture out of consumer complacency by throwing the culture right back into everybody's face, but Observationalists charm a culture out of its stupor by regaling them with chucklesome jokes about cookie packaging, sullen 7-Eleven clerks, and muffler repair shops. Pop artists banalized the monumental and monumentalized the banal. Observationalists banalize the banal and ignore the monumental completely—and offer a good deal of amusement in the process. In return we give them sitcoms, fame, large bank accounts, and a fair whack of allegiance.

The current hegemony of observational comedy most likely owes its existence to four factors:

1) Media supersaturation of American culture

2) Consumer abundance in American culture

3) American fascination with technology and

4) The rise and rise of the comedy club in heartland America during the eighties.

If one travels back in time, antecedents to modern, what's-the-deal-with ...? style comedy may exist in the form of, say, Sid Caesar, Bill "Pudding-Pops" Cosby, and David Brenner. It was only with the eighties convergence of all four above

Bill Cosby

I remember as a kid I used to love horror pictures with Frankenstein, Wolfman, the Mummy. The Mummy and Frankenstein were my two favorites. They would scare me to death. But now as I look at them as a grownup, I said "gee, whiz, anybody they catch really deserves to die." Cuz they are without a doubt the two slowest *monsters in the world.*

Bill Cosby
The Best on Record, *1965*

components, however, that observational comedy became the defining comedy of the present era.

First, media:

Will Rogers once sat onstage and merely read aloud the day's paper, having his audience pee in its pants with laughter—possibly the first known incidence of media-related observational comedy. Of course, Will Rogers did this routine many decades ago. Surviving modern newspapers must fight for brain time with TV shows, cable shows, movies, Blockbuster video rentals, infomercials, magazines, and scent strips as well as satellite dishes and . . . well . . . everything. Regardless of what curmudgeons and naysayers would have you believe, we'll soon live on a planet where everybody alive has grown up with TV. Information density and TV awareness spawns its own sensibility, and this sensibility tends to be the observational sensibility. Think of the Carson monologues slipping into the era of Leno and Letterman. Observation tends to be ironic, and irony is a device for making ludicrous situations palatable—for connecting the seeming randomness of televised discontinuity to a deeper, previously absent subconscious. Yet while irony is aloof, observation is inclusive. Good observation puts politics aside. A good observational comic asks you, "What's the deal with white Volkswagen convertibles; Snuggle, the fabric softener bear; gloss versus semigloss; and *Three's Company* reruns?" and then gives you the answer.

Second, consumer abundance:

Observational humor is distinctly American. A pivotal defining aspect of both America and TV is the dream of effortless abundance. "What's the deal with raspberry-flavored fluoride rinses at the dentist?" or, "What's the deal with fresh-squeezed versus freshly squeezed?" When politics becomes somewhat beside the point, observation reigns. All issues become personal and we enter the realm of deep contemplation of cereal boxes, StairMasters, and 96-ounce slush-type beverages. Like it or not, we now live in a world where gargantuan and terrifying consumer entities land in our midst like UFOs—bulk shopping outlets, strip malls, and TV channels that sell only zirconium rings. The observational comedian helps the audience to understand these UFOs—he or she becomes a kind of user's manual to all the inflections of laissez-faire abundance. Observationalists zero in on some fantastically arcane and minute dimension of everyday life which, upon articulation, is then rendered harmless. A good observational comic will ask the audience, "What's the deal with a car air freshener shaped like Mr. T?" and then gives the audience the answer. And the audience says "thank you."

Third, technology:

We love technology, and technology loves us. Or, well, sort of. We made the

DAVID BRENNER

Whenever I am asked about a monumental moment on TV, I always select my first appearance on The Tonight Show *because it was my TV debut and led to all that was to follow. However, this time I want to tell you about my first and only time on* The Ed Sullivan Show. *Why was it my only? Was I that lousy? Did I give someone the finger?*

I calmly stood backstage. Ed Sullivan introduced me. I walked through the curtain, hit my spot, and performed my monologue. As with my Tonight Show *appearance, I even ad-libbed a couple lines. Every line elicited uproarious laughter and/or enthusiastic applause. As we comedians say—It was a killer, out of the ballpark, home run! When I ended, the audience went wild. Ed Sullivan had no choice but to call me back out onstage. This was a first in the history of the show. I had scored such a TV first only a couple weeks previously in my* Tonight Show *debut, but this was LIVE! This was ED SULLIVAN! Ed Sullivan came over, shook my hand, signaled to the audience, which was still applauding wildly. I kept thanking the audience and glanced up at the TV stage monitor to catch a glimpse of the legendary Ed Sullivan with his arm around my shoulder, hand extended to the studio audience and the millions of Americans in their homes witnessing this unique comedy moment. What I saw was not this wonderful image and lifetime memory. What I saw was a box of Preparation H. After my last joke, they had gone to a commercial. No one outside the theater had seen the moment.*

But the powers had seen it, and immediately there was talk about a contract for three additional appearances. Unfortunately, before the contract could be signed, CBS decided to cancel The Ed Sullivan Show. *I had the distinction of being the last comedian to appear on the last live* Ed Sullivan Show.

The postscript to this story is also ironic. When David Letterman made the move to CBS, he asked me to be a guest on his first show. So, I, the last comedian to walk off the stage of The Ed Sullivan Theater, became the first comedian to walk back on that same stage twenty-three years later. Yes, I hit it out of the ballpark, but this time, instead of no one in America seeing my encore, no one even saw a moment of me. As with most first week shows, it didn't make it to air!

stuff, so it can only ever be a reflection of ourselves. So our relationship with technology gives us a healthy litmus test of our relationship with ourselves. We are the machines we build. Enter the Observationalist. Do you ever speak with coworkers via Post-it Notes? Have you ever willfully left a message on someone's answering machine hoping they wouldn't answer the phone? Does on-line anything ever enter your daydreams? Shelley Berman and Bob Newhart both articulated the absurdities implicit in technology back in the fifties with their highlightings of telephones; Alan King and Stan Freberg fed on airlines. But only now, with the help of 680X0 microprocessors, ludicrously cheap petroleum, and a media obsessed with a vaporishly existent information highway can the modern Observationalist

---

I think the funniest fans of all have to be golf fans. I mean that's a great sport. The guy hits the ball and then all the fans follow him. Could you see that like in baseball? A guy gets a hit, "Okay everyone, first base! Come on!"

David Brenner
The Tonight Show, *1981*

Cats run away. My wife's cat ran away for three days, sending me out in the middle of the night driving around looking for the cat—like the cat's going to stick to the main road.

Jay Leno
The Tonight Show, *1986*

Bob Newhart peforming in 1960

Bob Newhart on *The Hollywood Palace* (1964–67, 1970)

Newhart (1982–90)

George Carlin in a 1976 appearance at the Roxy on Sunset Strip, Hollywood

explore the intricacies of honey-roasted airline giveaway peanuts, hotel voice mail, photocopiers, freeways, in-car beverage holders, and cable company uselessness. In the same way that we slap a Richter number onto an earthquake as soon as possible to make it seem as if we're in control of the earthquake, the Observationalist slaps a what's-the-deal-with? on some irritating new invention, thus rendering it cute, harmless, and mundane. When the world is too much for us, we don't necessarily head for the *Wall Street Journal. Caroline's Comedy Hour* can sometimes offer a more plausible focus to the confused. A successful Observationalist will ask his audience, "What's the deal with 1–900 numbers for adult diaper enthusiasts?" and then provide the audience with the answer.

Fourth, comedy clubs:

Somewhere in the early eighties, comedy clubs began their now historic process of popularization, supersaturation, Darwinian winnowing, and stabilization. This ultimately led America to the point where most of its cities now have at least three clubs called "Chuckle McBean's," "The Laff Connection," or "The Smile Emporium." Comedy clubs, in their own way, became the zeitgeist puppy mills of their era. One has only to look at a crackly old rental video of a very very young Jerry Seinfeld, or Sandra Bernhard, or Ellen DeGeneres not only to sniffle wistfully at how young we all once were, but to see just how sophisticated the observational sensibility has become. We also see how much of a crèche the comedy clubs and the subsequent cable comedy shows these clubs spawned actually were. The eighties comedy club explosion forced literally tens of thousands of aspiring comedians to ask the question, "Is material finite?" Observation triumphed. Observation has, in TV sitcoms, if not replaced character as a central component, certainly become a necessary adjunct. Witness *Frasier, Seinfeld, Ellen, Friends,* et al. In the old comedy club tapes, we can see the stars of today honing their abilities to bridge seamlessly from topic to topic, mimicking the connective bridges of TV laugh tracks and music, avoiding those jagged edges that give an audience anxiety. In the end, the seamless genre spawned by TV filtered through the clubs and back into the world of TV. The good observational comedian asks, "What's the deal with all these comedy clubs?" and then gives the audience an answer.

Observational stand-up is not vaudeville. It is not USO. It's not *Laugh-In.* Envision a Bob Hope joke about Zsa Zsa Gabor circa 1960, and the antiquity of previous comedy genres becomes evident. The modern Observationalist's targets are clear: McDonald's, 7-Eleven, twisted coworkers, oddly marketed products, trashy neighborhoods, CNN, best-if-used-before disclaimers, deodorants. The list, like the array of effluvia created by modern times, is endless.

I think God may not be perfect. I think his work shows that. Take a look at a mountain range: they're all crooked, they're never in line, all different sizes, there are no two leaves the same—he can't even give two people the same fingerprints! He's had billions of years to work on this stuff. And everything he has ever made—died. Everything? So far.

George Carlin
Saturday Night Live, *1975*

Jerry Seinfeld

Ellen DeGeneres

Fleas, they have no beneficial reason at all to be here, and I always thought at times like this, when we can't figure things out for ourselves, wouldn't it be great if we could just pick up the phone and call up God, and ask him these things . . . "Yeah, hi God, it's Ellen . . . Look there are certain things on this earth, I just don't understand why they're here . . . I was thinking more about, um, fleas. Fleas have no beneficial reason at all to . . . um . . . no, I didn't realize how many people are employed by the flea collar industry. Not to mention sprays. Well, I guess you're right, 'Course you are! 'Course you are! Yah, being who you are . . . ."

Ellen DeGeneres
The 5th Annual American Comedy
Awards, *1991*

How many times do you feel that, you feel that, you know, that, "I gotta get out," right? "I gotta get out." And you go out, you stand around somewhere for a little while, and you go, "I gotta be getting back. . . . I've been out, I've got to get back, I've got to go to sleep, I've got to get up, I've got to go out again tomorrow." That is the feeling of life: you've gotta go. All the time. You get to your job; what is your first thought? I wanna get home. Once you get home, you feel cooped up, you gotta get out. You're out, it's late, you gotta get back. Wherever you are, you've gotta get the hell out of there.

Jerry Seinfeld
Jerry Seinfeld's Stand-Up Confidential
1987

You know where I like to shop? Those big warehouse stores, like BJ's and Price Club. They're great. I get a flatbed and just wheel it around there. Oooh. Give me some big stuff. And you know, everybody goes there to buy the same thing. Everybody goes there to buy that big eighteen-roll toilet paper thing. It's the cheapest toilet paper on the planet. It's got wood chunks in that toilet paper. Trees are growing out of there, furry animals nesting. Two cents, eighteen rolls.

Cathy Ladman
One Night Stand, *1991*

Have you seen these Johnny Walker ads up they have around the city? Are these like the most annoying thing? I love this one: "He's crazy about my kid, and he drinks Johnny Walker." My, there's a winning combination.

Carol Leifer
Really Big Shoo!, *1990*

Once upon a time people used to while away their creative hours tying macrame jute owls onto snags of driftwood. Now they while away their hours creatively channel surfing. Observation has mirrored and followed this transition from whimsical participator to critical observer. Yet observational comedy has remained true-to-life, never exaggerated. Exaggeration would render true observation impotent. Premoistened towelettes are self-parodying, as are TV channels devoted solely to SoloFlex products and people who use cellular phones in the middle of your theatrical enjoyment of *Curly Sue.*

Observationalists provide universality in a period of what seems to be social fracture. Observationalists make it okay to be a member of the culture as it really is, not as ideologues would have you wish it were. The Observationalist is your tour guide—somebody who, like you, is stranded, Gulliverlike, in this world of silly things gone sillyishly cuckoo. In the old days, artists worked hard to manufacture the surreal; nowadays our culture is preprogrammed to manufacture only surrealistic constructs and objects. Observationalists validate these absurd parking tickets of modern existence—these Magritte paintings we now call life. I am he as we are me, and we are she, and we are all *together*, and yes, we're all stuck with premoistened towelettes.

That's the deal.

Rita Rudner

Beneath the Fringe:
A Glossary for the Modern Audience

by Merle Kessler

ENTERTAINMENT/ENTERTAINED: A DEFINITION

Manipulation; symbiosis; mild mutual contempt.

RESISTANCE TO COMEDY

In America's early days, theatricality was suspect among certain of our Christian brethren. "Did Jesus go to shows?" they asked, rhetorically. "We rest our case." Early audiences consisted of drunken godless yokels with loaded weapons. (In other respects they were ideal. They didn't tithe. This gave them disposable incomes, necessary for any popular entertainment to flourish.)

STAND-UP

A person tries to elicit laughter from frequently hostile strangers.
This is, in itself, fringe behavior.

TELLING STAND-UP TERMS

"I died." "I killed."

THE BIRTH OF STAND-UP

The roots of stand-up lie in the nineteenth-century minstrel show. An interlocutor (ancestor of the "straight man") fed setups to "Tambo" and "Bones," who provided punch lines full of "gwines" and "massas." Minstrel shows were performed by white people in blackface. When black people were finally tolerated onstage, they also had to disguise themselves with burnt cork. Black people pretending to be black people: how fringe can you get?

RADIO CITY, MOVIELAND, GANGLAND

Comics roamed the countryside, downloading *shtick* at glamorous performance palaces in small towns across America. Vaudevillians brought a taste of the city to the farm: dialect jokes, leering at large blonde women, secular songs. Rubes were their meal tickets, their demographic, their fans.

Then hicks began to stay home with the radio. Performance palaces became movie houses. Prohibition seized the country by its scrawny throat. The city, in retaliation, became a concrete dreamland of hoods, flappers, hoofers, and private eyes, lit only by the neon of the Great White Way. "From now on," urban America

Sandra Bernhard

growled to the rube out of the side of its mouth, "if you wanna drink the bathtub gin, you gotta know the password."

There was more going on in the urban underbelly than radio and movies could possibly show. The city got hep, which begat hip, which begat cool, which begat postmodern.

Jazz: music so cool only the urban dweller could appreciate it. Broadway faltered. Nighthawks stumbled down mean streets, lit only by scattered streetlights. Mobbed-up slickers smoked stogies the size of baseball bats, as they squired major blondes into seedy joints. Take that, Square John!

Las Vegas arose from the desert like the hallucination of a speed freak phoenix. With Vegas as its dim beacon, the fifties displayed America's dark underworld: full of Percodan, juvenile delinquents, unfiltered cigarettes, and the Rat Pack. We got *Playhouse 90* and *77 Sunset Strip*, cement overshoes and convertibles, scandal rags and blackmail schemes. Stand-up festered in its new environment.

Lenny Bruce, in his early days, opening for strippers in some smoke-filled mob joint, once came onstage naked for a laugh. The mob was not amused. Comedy was one thing, nakedness another.

SOME BEGATS AND DEATHS: A RECAP

The minstrel show begat burlesque, which begat vaudeville, which killed burlesque. Burlesque devolved into girlie shows, then, finally, porno.

Vaudeville begat radio and movies, which plundered vaudeville.

Radio begat television.

A TRUTH WE OFTEN FORGET

The early comedy stars of radio, television, and movies had their roots in vaudeville. A rule of showbiz: yesterday's fringe is today's mainstream. Chevy Chase *is* Bob Hope. Another rule: strippers never leave the fringe.

THE FIFTIES

With some exceptions (Ernie Kovacs), the television comedy scene was ruled by vaudevillians or people like them (*The Ed Sullivan Show*, Lucille Ball, Sid Caesar).

But something else was happening. *Mad* magazine. Mort Sahl. The Compass Players. Second City. Lenny Bruce. *Improv*. Beatniks. Button-down shirts. Martinis. Bad chianti. Jack Kerouac. Wise-ass college kids demanding to be taken seriously as humorous people. Steve Allen. Jonathan Winters! Oh joy!

John Kennedy provided an uneasy interface between beatniks and the mob.

THE SIXTIES

When President Kennedy was assassinated, Mort Sahl stopped being funny.

Thanks to Vietnam and television censors, the Smothers Brothers (a brother act: pure vaudeville) no longer felt like being funny.

In San Francisco, the Committee became an improv collective. What would Karl Marx have thought?

Though Richard Pryor and George Carlin burned their blazers and let their hair grow, comedy in general suffered. When your audience is listening to the Moody Blues with its mouth hanging open, it's hard to create a humor database. Low points: *Laugh-In, The Dean Martin Show.*

A SIXTIES ANECDOTE

In the late sixties, I attended a girlie show at my local county fair. I expected a perfunctory discarding of skimpy clothing. But it wasn't even that classy. The former Miss June Sixty-Two pranced into the tent to the strains of *Goldfinger,* wearing nothing but the frost on her smile.

A bunch of guys stood around on the dirt floor, separated from her by a length of frayed rope. A man stood in the rear behind us, moving around, looking for the best vantage point, his grin as glazed as hers. He was a farmer, a rube, the same age I am now, wearing bib overalls.

Some half century earlier, a rube like him would have had to listen to a comic croak off-color jokes before he could watch the lady remove her flimsies. Those days were gone. In the sixties, we downsized the entertainment package. Cut to the chase: forget the comedy, the clothes. Enter naked, give the rubes a thrill, and get out.

Was comedy dead?

THE SEVENTIES

Comedy came into its own. It took awhile for the laughs to kick in, because all of us (except Republicans) were discovering ourselves, and were totally humorless about the process.

But it did happen: *National Lampoon, Saturday Night Live, Animal House,* Richard Pryor, *Monty Python,* Robin Williams, Steve Martin . . . .

TYPES OF MODERN COMEDY: A PRIMER

Vaudeville's ghost

Jerry Lewis began his career by mugging onstage to pop songs. In 1945, he and crooner Dean Martin were booked separately at a Manhattan mob joint;

Reiner: Sir, to live as long as you have, to stay healthy and live this long, you must have some secrets of life.

Brooks: I have a couple secrets.

Reiner: Would you tell us? We'd be very interested in hearing it.

Brooks: Well, if you want to live to 2,000 years you don't touch fried food.

Reiner: You don't eat fried food.

Brooks: No. And you don't run for a bus. You stroll. Jaunty-jolly, with your hat at a rakish tilt, one leg after the other, strolling to the bus.

Reiner: Well sir, that's not quite enough to stay alive for 2,000 years, not eating fried foods and strolling jaunty-jolly. There must be something else.

Brooks: Yes, that's true. There is another thing.

Reiner: What is that?

Brooks: Luck. Without luck, you're dead. You need a lot of luck.

Mel Brooks and Carl Reiner
The Ed Sullivan Show: "The 2,000-Year-Old Man," 1961

Dean Martin and Jerry Lewis

Lily Tomlin

Why is it that when we're talking to God, we're said to be praying, but when God talks to us we're schizophrenic?

Lily Tomlin
Standing Room Only: Lily Tomlin in Appearing Nitely, *1979*

I refuse to be intimidated by reality any more. What is reality? Nothing but a collective hunch.

Lily Tomlin
The First Annual American Comedy Awards, *1987*

they started kibitzing in each other's acts. The rest is history.

Andy Kaufman used to do a pantomime to the theme from *Mighty Mouse.* Most drag acts have their roots in pantomime. A dim phantom, vaudeville walks among us.

Neo-vaudeville

Saturday Night Live's "wild and crazy guys" and *Taxi*'s Latka Gravas upgraded vaudeville's dialect humor. Today, a dialect mocked must be from an imaginary

Steven Wright

Andy Kaufman

Curiosity killed the cat—but for a while I was the suspect. . . . Why is the alphabet in that order? Is it because of that song? . . . If I melt dry ice, can I swim without getting wet? . . . I stayed up all night playing poker with Tarot cards—I got a full house and four people died. . . . When I was little, in our backyard we had a quicksand box. I was an only child—eventually. . . . One time the police stopped me for speeding and they said, "You know the speed limit is 55 miles an hour," and I said, "Yeah, I know, but I wasn't going to be out that long." . . . I hate when my foot falls asleep during the day, because that means it's going to be up all night. . . . I put instant coffee into a microwave oven—I almost went back in time. . . . It's a small world, but I wouldn't want to paint it.

Steven Wright
A Steven Wright Special, 1985

country, so nobody is offended. Similarly, we no longer have Stepin Fetchits being a-scared of ghosts; robots fill that function.

Neo-button-down

Bill Maher and Dennis Miller. One wears a necktie, the other doesn't.

The formerly smoke-filled room

Though fallen from public favor, there must be scores of comics named Shecky out there, still spritzing after all these years. Nowadays, the spritzers want respect, to jump from the toilets to Broadway. The act can no longer survive as a string of gags: it's a one-man show, an HBO special.

The eternal frat

Saturday Night Live, "Dice" Clay. Boys will always be boys.

Bizarro world

Andy Kaufman, Steven Wright, Jonathan Winters, Albert Brooks. I once saw Albert Brooks on *The Tonight Show* dressed as a mime, complete with whiteface, tights, and little painted teardrop. Then he did a completely straight stand-up routine. I was on the floor. Don't ask me why.

The edge

Sam Kinison brought evangelical fervor to his secular act. Denis Leary defiantly smoked onstage, and made jokes about eating red meat. What a rebel.

"Is it just me, or . . . ?"

Andy Rooney and Jerry Seinfeld make whimsical observations about pencils and household appliances.

"We're working through some personal issues"

"Anybody out there in therapy?"

"We're young and kind of angry but not enough to put you off"

Def Comedy Jam, Martin Lawrence, Margaret Cho.

Pomo

In the postmodern world, successful comics pretend to despise what they're doing (David Letterman). Attitude is everything. One must not only be self-conscious, but share self-consciousness with the audiences: Garry Shandling does *The Larry Sanders Show*, a comedy about a comedian.

Funny lists, once the mainstay of bourgeois humor ("You know you're middle-aged when . . . ," "Happiness is . . .") are now hip. Jim Carrey is a Jerry Lewis waiting for France to discover him.

Duck's Breath Mystery Theatre troupe: Leon Martell, Dan Coffey, Bill Allard, Merle Kessler, and Jim Turner

MAKE 'EM LAUGH, MAKE 'EM LAUGH: A FRINGE ANECDOTE

Back in the late seventies, Duck's Breath Mystery Theatre* once performed in what could aptly be called a hellhole. We were in the middle of shouting our way through a silly sketch called "How to Carry Chairs," secure in the belief that none of the boisterous tools of Satan in attendance were watching.

Suddenly, we were proven wrong. An audience member picked up a chair and started screaming, "Here's how you carry a %*&#@ chair, you *&$@#s!" He smashed it on the floor and stood quivering with rage.

We were worried for a moment. But his synapse-free colleagues continued shouting at each other and drinking heavily, not paying him (or us) the least bit of attention. Even the rage-filled one, though not diminished in his anger one whit, transferred his gaze to a spot on the wall and stood glaring at that. Relieved, we soldiered on.

---

* *The author is a cofounder of* Duck's Breath Mystery Theatre, *with whom he performed on stage, radio, television, and film from 1975 to 1990.*

Steve Martin at Nassau Coliseum, Long Island, New York (1978)

Monty Python's Flying Circus (1969–74) members Terry Jones, Eric Idle, Graham Chapman, Michael Palin, and John Cleese

I had, a couple of months ago, a very important experience in my life and I'd like to share it with you. I went to France, and I visited the cathedral at Chartres, and I had a very moving experience. If you've never seen it, it's a magnificent building, probably 400 years old, beautiful stained glass, and I have to be honest with you: I was very, very moved. And as I was writing my name on it with a can of spray paint, I thought of something I read about a year ago that has completely changed my life. And tonight I would like to share this with you. It's not often in literature that you come across a phrase or sentence that really means a lot to you, and I'd like to read this to you right now. [Takes a piece of paper from his pocket]: Apply to infested area.

Steve Martin
Saturday Night Live*, 1978*

THE EIGHTIES

Belushi died. *Ghostbusters*. Steve Martin, Eddie Murphy: superstars.

Cable television realized that if it gathered several stand-ups, stuck them in front of a brick wall, and videotaped them—presto, it had itself a program. And it only cost a dollar!

THE END OF COMEDY AS WE KNOW IT?

When Andy Kaufman died of cancer in the early eighties, I thought it was one of his jokes. A friend who'd seen him perform told me he came out singing "99 Bottles of Beer on the Wall" to an increasingly hostile audience. But when he stopped at "two bottles" and left the stage, the audience went crazy trying to bring him back to finish the song. Go figure.

BYE-BYE TO MY END OF THE FRINGE

Despite our muddled efforts, Duck's Breath eventually achieved a certain amount of fame. Our material stayed pretty much the same (baggy pants filled with dada),

Did you ever look at Don King and think that he might be Buckwheat's illegitimate child?

Robin Williams
Catch a Rising Star 10th Anniversary
Special, *1982*

Robin Williams (in character as an old "crazy" man from the future): *That's my only love: crazy. Because there's no way any government in the world can handle madness. 'Cause you got to fly above it all. Remember, angels, they have wings 'cause they take themselves lightly.*

Robin Williams
On Location: Robin Williams: Off the
Wall, *1978*

but we slowly became respectable, probably because of our intermittent presence on National Public Radio. The *Village Voice* wrote up one of our final shows, saying something like "America's not funny any more, and Duck's Breath knows it." We would have preferred something like "Mile-a-minute yuckathon! Catch them before Hollywood does!" But no. The *Village Voice* does not do blurbs—another cruel show business lesson we learned, alas, too late.

AN INSTRUCTIVE POSTMODERN STAND-UP EXPERIENCE

One afternoon in the early eighties, I happened to catch *The Mike Douglas Show*. Mike's guests included Devo, the defunct fringe band, and some Vegas comic. The Devo members wore jumpsuits and little red pyramids on their heads, for some reason (no doubt artistic). The comic wore a sports coat with lapels so wide it looked like it might fly away. The comic began to ad-lib (what show people did before improvisation), in which mode he suggested that Devo's pyramids were Dolly Parton's bra cups. Mike Douglas roared. Devo looked terrified and confused.

Now the pop quiz:

Was Devo trying to be funny with the pyramid hats? The Vegas comic *was* trying to be funny. Was he though? Who was funny? Who was just bizarre?

Evaluate. Discuss.

THE NINETIES

Twice in as many years in the course of my solo career, a career so checkered it can cause hallucinations if viewed too closely, I heard television producers describe the viewers of their programs as "morons." I was asked to adjust my humor accordingly.

MAKE 'EM LAUGH, MAKE 'EM LAUGH II: A FRINGE ANECDOTE CONTINUED

The term backstage doesn't do justice to the mildewed zone in which we made our costume changes. Backstage was a narrow corridor between two unisex bathrooms lit by one red lightbulb just above head level. As I tugged on my trousers for another humorous sketch, an intense thin lad with pupils large as quarters stumbled past me, saw the red lightbulb, snarled, reached up, and crushed it in his hand. Thankfully, he didn't transfer his hatred of illumination to me.

We got paid fifty bucks for our efforts, and in further compensation the club owner was later sent to prison on a manslaughter rap. But we mainly earned that mysterious thing called "chops." We were learning how to create humor for that common denominator a step below the lowest.

Robin Williams

JONATHAN WINTERS

Probably the most fun of all the guys—I would say this strongly for all of you who stay up late—was Johnny Carson. I miss Carson. I liked him because he had little depart-ments, like Steve Allen; whether they were great, fair, bad, it didn't make a difference. He took chances and I think that's a very important part of this business.

Before the show Johnny would say to me, "What do you want to talk about tonight?" And I would say, "I want to talk about growing up on a farm." And then I'd sit down there on that funny seat and he would say, "Jonathan, you were born on a farm outside of Dayton." "Yeah, my dad was an alcoholic, so we bought a farm, about 125 acres, that had hoof-and-mouth disease up front. Did you ever have to milk a cow lying down? We sold a lot of dead milk. People never died but they didn't go to work for a while."

But that was it. Johnny would be on the floor because he was a fan. I'd do a lot of shows where I'd come out and do my monologues, but on Carson I felt like I had finally arrived. It was just coming out and being able to sit with him and just talk.

If we'd simply marched around the stage that night shrieking and making fart noises, we would've *killed*. I know that now. On the other hand, a similar act played for one's mom would bring a frown of disapproval.

To make a living doing comedy on the fringe, I've learned, you must first pick your audience. Ask Howard Stern. Ask Rush Limbaugh. With the right demo-graphics, being on the fringe doesn't matter. If you're going to build a cult follow-ing, in other words, make sure it has a disposable income.

THE MILLENNIUM

The modern comic leaves stand-up as soon as possible. It's a means to an end, an extended audition for a fabulous future: a sitcom! A glamorous film career! You can enjoy a long slowly fading career, surrounded by bodyguards as you reject movie scripts and play golf.

Who needs live performance, with its endless parade of in-your-face actual people you have to please? Who needs to pursue a laugh, when a network, a stu-dio, or marketing will do that for you?

The World of Jonathan Winters (1965; unaired pilot)

Battle of the Sexes

by Anne Beatts

"Take my wife, please." A line so memorable that when a chunky, owlish, fiddle-playing comedian with a sexually ambivalent first name—Henny—first uttered it on the *The Ed Sullivan Show* it became a catchphrase to describe an entire comedic style.

It's important to bear in mind that in order for "take my wife, please" to be funny first someone had to say, "take my wife." And that after Henny Youngman added the "please," no one could say "take my wife" ever again without the ghost of a please floating in the air.

Henny's routine went further than simply suggesting he wanted to rid himself of his wife. He also explained why: "My wife has a nice even disposition—miserable all the time. You know, my wife went to the beauty parlor. She got a mud pack. She looked nice for a couple of days. Then the mud fell off."

Rodney Dangerfield weighed in on the same subject: "My wife ran after the garbage truck this morning. Too bad they waved her off." And Alan King summed it all up with: "Women live longer than men—there's a reason. They're not married to women."

Liberated women who mutinied against the "take my wife, please" school of comedy in the seventies may not have known or remembered another Sullivan regular, a small blonde woman in a poodle cut and an evening gown. Jean Carroll gave as good as she got: "My husband drinks to steady his nerves. The other night they got so steady he couldn't move at all. In fact, he had a little accident—he was going from a nightclub to his car and someone stepped on his hand."

But whichever side of the fence you squared off on, back in the days of Ed's "reely big shew," the battle lines of the war between men and women were clearly drawn. Men were alcohol-guzzling, sports-obsessed Neanderthals, and women were ditzy goofballs who drove with one hand out the window so you couldn't tell if they were signaling or just drying their nail polish.

Then along came a breath of fresh, impudent air: Phyllis Diller. A tiny dynamo, she had a mouth that wouldn't quit and a shock of hair that made her look, according to her mate, the much-maligned Fang, like "a lion that's bit into an electric Christian." She grabbed hold of the stereotypes and shook them till they rattled. She made fun of her own driving. She hated cooking and housework: "I don't like to cook. I can make a TV dinner taste like radio."

On *The Beautiful Phyllis Diller Show*, she showed us a kind of female star we'd never seen before: a sloppy loudmouth in a fright wig whose ever-present cigarette

Home Improvement (debuted in 1991) with Tim Allen and Patricia Richardson

Jill: Remember what we were talking about last night?

Tim: Oh, the baby. I won't bring it up again, promise.

Jill: I'm bringing it up. C'mon, haven't you thought about how nice it would be to have a little girl?

Tim: No! We have all the kids we can stand right now.

Jill: We never actually said that we weren't going to have another baby.

Tim: I've said it, I've talked about it, I know I've talked about it, I mentioned it on Tool Time.

Jill: Oh great, so eleven people know about it?

Tim: You remember babies at all? Dirty diapers, colic, 2 A.M. feedings, 3 A.M. feedings. I don't have the energy for that anymore.

Jill: You don't have the energy to say "wake up Jill, the baby wants you"?

Tim Allen
Home Improvement, *1993*

My wife, the way she throws away money, it's ridiculous, you know? I mean, who tips at a toll booth? She don't care about nothing, my wife. Wants me to take her out all the time, that's all. This afternoon she started with me. She said, "Take me someplace I've never been before." I took her to the kitchen.

Rodney Dangerfield
On Location with Rodney Dangerfield
1980

Oh, I feel so much better now, I had an awful night. I had a nightmare. I dreamt that Marilyn Monroe and my wife had a fight over me and my wife won. Now the funny thing is, my wife looks like the closest thing to Marilyn Monroe. She looks like Arthur Miller. Marilyn Monroe, take away her long blonde hair and what have you got? The sexiest bald-headed woman in the world.

Henny Youngman
The Ed Sullivan Show, *1959*

Rodney Dangerfield—"It's Not Easy Bein' Me" (1986)

holder sprinkled ashes like a benediction on lousy homemakers everywhere. She took the fifties ideal of Donna Reed and stuffed it in a smoke-filled oven along with her ringing phone.

Meanwhile, who knew what kind of housekeeper Phyllis Diller actually was in real life? She was perhaps the last comedienne who could still distance herself from her comic persona by saying, "But, seriously, though." The next wave of comics, both male and female, were anxious to erase that gap. What was going on in their daily lives was what shaped their material: their everyday experience, filtered through their unique comic sensibilities.

Henny Youngman on the comedy special *Just for Laughs*

Phyllis Diller

"Truth!" Joan Rivers says. "We believed you shouldn't do mother-in-law jokes if you didn't have a mother-in-law. Truth! I was the first woman to talk about orgasm on the stage . . . gynecology on the stage . . . subjects women had never spoken about before."

Joan also did jokes that Phyllis Diller or even Jean Carroll might have done: "Housework is futile—you make the bed, you do the dishes—six months later you have to do it all again." But she personalized them. As a result we took her self-deprecation seriously. When Jean Carroll said she was a lousy housekeeper, we laughed. When Phyllis Diller said it, we roared. When Joan Rivers said it, we laughed—and we believed her. The comic posture of self-loathing threatened to become disturbingly real.

No one better demonstrates the pitfalls of merging private and public personas than Woody Allen. By making his life into his art, Woody Allen invited his audience into both. The angst-filled, tortured, guilt-ridden, yet sexually voracious, wisecracking intellectual of his early TV and film appearances is inextricably enmeshed in the public mind with the angst-filled, not-all-that-tortured-or-guilt-ridden, sexually voracious suitor of Mia and Soon Yi.

Yet Woody Allen created "Woody Allen" telling jokes that, leaving out the references to Bergman and Kierkegaard, aren't all that different from the jokes told by Henny or Rodney or any of the other, older comedians whose names end in "y." Compare and contrast the following. Woody: "Sex and death. . . . They both only come once in my lifetime. And at least after death, you're not nauseous." Rodney Dangerfield: "The first time I had sex I was so scared—of course I was scared, I was all alone." The difference is in the delivery: nervous stuttering instead of Catskill-style tummeling.

If his predecessors were by turns irritated and bemused by the opposite sex, Woody Allen seemed to alternate between insatiable lust and abject terror—and thus escalated the conflict. Women were no longer simply mysterious, they were incomprehensible.

Incomprehensibly, many women found this posture sexually stimulating. Countless bespectacled thin-chested young men got laid throughout the sixties and seventies by passing themselves off as "a Woody Allen type." Today, the small screen is populated by Woody Allen types: Jerry Seinfeld, Richard Lewis, Garry Shandling. They've adopted the kvetching but not the Kierkegaard references: Woody Allen lite.

And Tim Allen, modern heir apparent to the exaggerated macho posturing of Jackie Gleason, is nowadays usually the one who gets sent to the moon by a spouse. Witness the following exchange. Tim: "Subtle? My middle name is subtle."

Jean Carroll

We all want a good relationship, we're willing to try, we all want to give the other person what they want, don't we? Trouble is, what does anybody want? Who knows? What do women want? Women want someone who . . . women want someone.

Men want to be really, really, really close to someone—who will leave them alone.

Elayne Boosler
Live Nude Girls, *1991*

One night I asked Fang to kiss me good-night, he got up and put on his work clothes. . . . I put on a peekaboo blouse, he peeked and booed. . . . His idea of a seven-course dinner is a six-pack and a bologna sandwich. Last time I said "Let's eat out," we ate in the garage.

Phyllis Diller
The Flip Wilson Show, *1971*

Jamie: I just don't know why this is all so hard.

Paul: What?

Jamie: This, everything, marriage, it's supposed to be different than this.

Paul: Says who?

Jamie: Everyone.

Paul: Well they're wrong, it's just like this. It's exactly like this.

Jamie: According to who?

Paul: Everybody. I asked around. Look, there's always going to be stuff. You know, I put up with your crap and you put up with my crap.

Jamie: That's marriage?

Paul: That's what I'm thinking.

Paul Reiser
Mad About You, *1992*

Quite often I've been asked in interviews, what are my views on women's liberation? And I think I feel good because I've finally considered the entire situation, I've got it clearly in focus and I say free 'em. Let 'em go.

Flip Wilson
The Flip Wilson Show, *1972*

Jill (Patricia Richardson): "Yeah. And your first name is 'not.'" *Home Improvement* even turns the myth of women drivers on its head when Tim accidentally drops a craneload of metal on Jill's car, crushing it. Like Ralph Kramden, Tim's character shares his most intimate moments not with his wife but with another man. But, in an ironic comment on male inability to achieve intimacy, Tim can only confide in his shadowy neighbor Wilson, whose full face is never seen on camera.

The classic comic pose of befuddlement is adopted by Paul Reiser in *Mad About You.* Jamie (Helen Hunt) rolls her eyes as Paul expounds his own brand of illogical logic: George Burns and Gracie Allen in reverse. Their view of marriage may be more equitable than Henny Youngman's: "Married for thirty years and I'm still in love with the same woman. If my wife ever found out, she'd kill me." But it is no more rosy. Paul: "I put up with your crap and you put up with my crap." Jamie: "That's marriage?" Paul: "That's what I'm thinking."

Meanwhile, if male comics, like characters in a Thurber cartoon, seem to be shrinking, comediennes are definitely expanding, trying on new styles and attitudes, some previously discarded by the men. Elayne Boosler harks back to the tradition of Will Rogers and Mort Sahl when she picks up a newspaper and gives her take on the news of the day. Rita Rudner applies the tentative cerebral style of Woody Allen to material that might have been delivered by Jean Carroll: "Men don't live well by themselves. They don't even live like people. They live like bears with furniture." And witness the spin Carol Leifer, as a woman, can put on the line "I don't have any children—that I know of."

Richard Lewis called Elayne Boosler "the Jackie Robinson of comedy." If so, then Roseanne is the Muhammad Ali. Despite our awareness of the real Roseanne as a multimillionaire who can afford all the plastic surgery she wants, she's completely convincing as blue-collar icon Roseanne Conner: "We are white trash, and we'll be white trash 'til the day they drag us to the curb."

For Roseanne, the battle of the sexes is over, and as the clear victor, she just needs to do some mopping-up on the battlefield. In one episode, she and her sister Jackie (Laurie Metcalf) felt so secure in their female power that Roseanne could actually pretend to be jealous of Jackie's husband Fred (Michael O'Keefe). Roseanne used her fake vulnerability like a judo move to throw Fred off balance and flip him around to her way of thinking. In Roseanne's world, Roseanne always wins. Phyllis Diller would be proud.

And in a world without Roseanne, there would be no *Grace Under Fire.* Brett Butler as Grace gets to play a divorced single mom who's funny, savvy, and sexy— without being punished for it. Reaching back into the past for male equivalents, an unlikely name turns up: Bob Cummings, the bachelor-on-the-make of *Love That*

Paul Reiser and Helen Hunt in *Mad About You* (debuted in 1992)

I've been married for five years now, which is quite an achievement in Hollywood. In Hollywood, when you meet a man, the first question you ask yourself is, "I don't know, is this the man I want my children to spend their weekends with?"

Rita Rudner
The 8th Annual American Comedy Awards, *1994*

I met a new girl. I met a girl at a barbecue, which was exciting. A beautiful girl. Blonde, I think—I don't know; her hair was on fire. . . . All she talked about was herself. You know those kinds of girls? I'm hot, I'm on fire—it was just me, me, me, you know. Help me. Put me out, you know.

Garry Shandling
The Garry Shandling Show 25th Anniversary Special, *1986*

Bob! His breezy charm provides a better analog than the stumblebum nature of the rest of TV's single males, from Fred MacMurray to John Larroquette.

Maybe because Brett Butler, following Joan Rivers's dictum—"Truth!"—has made her past history of spousal abuse not only public knowledge, but a touchstone of her comedy act, it's possible for the audience to forgive her freedom and her fast tongue. She doesn't merely want them to take her husband, please—he's already gone, and for a good reason.

These days Grace always gets the punch line, and a lot of her hits are directed below the belt of the male gender. In Russell the druggist (Dave Thomas), she has a goofy single male of her own always available for in-house torture. Yet their platonic friendship provides some of the strongest moments of the series. In the sexual wars these two have somehow forged an uneasy truce.

It's a trend. All over the dial, male and female characters who refrain from sleeping together are able to be friends: on *Seinfeld, Ellen,* and even *Friends.* It's a sign of the times. In the seventies, the mismatched roommates of shows like *Three's Company* didn't sleep together due to societal—and network—pressure. Now they just don't want to.

Think of it as a breather between sorties. The smoke may have cleared momentarily, but it seems inevitable that the age-old male-female conflict will not be resolved, in comedy or elsewhere, and that more shots will be fired from both sides. Such as this one: "These strangers in movies also fall in love the first time they ever have sex. Which is really weird, because I feel nothing but hatred and contempt." Woody Allen? No, Janeane Garofalo. It's a brick thrown through the window of the future. Take her sexual partner, please.

Roseanne (debuted in 1988) with John Goodman and Roseanne

A lot of stuff bugs me about husbands, you know, like, when they all the time want to talk to you—I hate that. Like he says, "Hey, Roseanne, don't you think we should talk about our sexual problems?" You know, like I'm gonna turn off Wheel of Fortune *for that. Put it on a gift certificate, babe.*

Roseanne
Funny, *1985*

Comics with Attitude: The Tough Guys

By Mel Watkins

Since the eighties, America's popular culture has been inundated by an assertive, in-your-face form of creative expression. Athletes prance and posture in the end zone after touchdowns or mockingly stare down their opponents after thunderous dunk shots; television and radio talk show hosts routinely ridicule and castigate callers and guests; and singers like Madonna or such gangsta rappers as N.W.A (Niggers with Attitude) openly flout traditional values about sex and violence and flaunt their disdain for authority. Controversy and shock are common stock in today's popular entertainment.

Nowhere is this more evident than in the world of stand-up comedy. During the past twenty years the comedy scene has witnessed the rise of a raft of comedians who insistently deliver their humor with a mixture of machismo, bile, and belligerence. Although their talent varies widely, the list of Tough Guys includes Richard Pryor, the late Sam Kinison, Eddie Murphy, Martin Lawrence, Denis Leary, Paul Mooney, and a gaggle of lesser-known comics who are regularly showcased on national television and in small clubs across the country.

Given the current allure of attitude and antiheroes, the popularity of these performers is not surprising. But, despite our present-day fascination, comedians with tough, assertive attitudes have been around for longer than we might imagine. In fact, they are not always tough "guys"; there have been a few tough gals as well.

Back in the thirties, for example, Mae West mesmerized her audiences with her combative demeanor and risqué remarks. Onstage and in films, she both startled and appalled fans with a steamy, rowdy comic persona that was unprecedented in popular entertainment at the time. She was best known for the sexual innuendo that pickled her stage act and her movie dialogue: "Come up and see me sometime," or "He's so old he can't take yes for an answer."

Even earlier, as a Ziegfeld Follies star, W. C. Fields was keeping audiences in stitches with his own brand of caustic humor. He often affected the pose of a beleaguered underdog, but it was his snappish retorts and churlishly aloof attitude that distinguished his comedy. Apparently, he could be equally uncivil offstage. One director called him "the most obstinate, ornery son of a bitch" he had ever

Eddie Murphy

Mike Douglas (at left) with Moms Mabley and Redd Foxx in 1973 on *The Mike Douglas Show*

worked with and legend has it that, when asked for a loan by a struggling actor, Fields replied, "I'd really like to help you, but I'm sorry I can't. All my money is tied up in cash."

By the forties a black comedienne was subtly spicing her monologues with suggestive commentary. She was primarily known as a folksy old matriarch, but behind her whimsical appearance lurked a peevish satirist. With a wink of the eye Moms Mabley often segued into an assertive blue humor that smacked of attitude. Her most famous quip, of course, is "there ain't nothin' an old man can do for me 'cept show me the way to a young one." But she was also adept at ridiculing society's pretense and absurdity: "I was ridin' along in my Cadillac, goin' through one of them little towns in South Carolina. Pass through a red light. One of them big cops come runnin' over to me, say, 'Hey woman, don't you know you went through a red light. . . . Well, what did you do that for?' I said 'Cause I seen all you white folks goin' on the green light. . . . I thought the red light was for us.'"

Still, the tough attitudes projected by West, Fields, and Mabley seem benign when compared with the direct assaults and more explicit language affected by the comedians who followed them. During the fifties, for example, Redd Foxx and Lenny Bruce began attracting the attention of large national audiences as well as critics and, often, the authorities. Bruce surfaced in San Francisco's hip North Beach area and, by 1957, was gaining recognition as a radical popular culture iconoclast. An habitué of those dingy, offbeat joints (or toilets as he and Foxx called them) where jazz musicians, hustlers, and strippers congregated, he absorbed the language and irreverent perceptions of that environment and combined them with his own intellectual disposition and a facile borscht circuit delivery.

Mirroring the netherworld of the black hipster that inspired his approach, he relentlessly attacked his audience's complaisant assumptions about sex, drugs, and other taboo subjects. "My mother-in-law broke up my marriage," he once remarked. "One day my wife came home early from work and found us in bed together. 'You're a pervert,' she said. 'Why,' I said, 'she's your mother, not mine.'"

Bruce's blasphemous comic persona disturbed American audiences more profoundly than any previously seen. It also led to his demise. Hounded by police and frequently jailed for obscenity, he found his career came to a virtual halt. Finally, ostracized and near crazed, he overdosed on heroin in 1966.

Redd Foxx, who admitted that "Lenny paved the way for all of us," avoided the persecution that plagued Bruce perhaps only because he was more flexible. During the fifties and the sixties he was known primarily for his blue humor and party records; he is mostly remembered now as the lovable old junk man he

I knew I wasn't going to college when I didn't get into high school. It didn't matter to me 'cos they weren't teaching nothing could help me now. "Little Boy Blue come blow your horn." Shit. You'll break your neck trying to blow your horn. You want your horn blown, you need a friend.

Redd Foxx
On Location, *1978*

Richard Pryor

portrayed in NBC's *Sanford and Son* (1972–77). In his stand-up act, however, he displayed something of the combative aura of his old friend Malcolm X.

He not only voiced the kind of shocking and profane comic insights that had made Bruce controversial, but also excelled at a type of insult humor that Don Rickles would make fashionable in the seventies. A loudmouth balcony patron at one performance elicited: "Why don't you rest yo' lips, nigger, you got a busy night ahead of you. This is your night in the barrel." Foxx's sly expressions, swaggering demeanor, and rapid-fire gags and put-downs were separated only by a hairline from images of the fast-talking, razor-toting black man that America had traditionally feared. And he reinforced that connection with jokes that cut much deeper than the funny bones of his audiences:

> *White people, quit moving around the country like a bunch of damned gypsies. Wherever you are, we'll be there.*

> *Would you rather see me up here or out in the park choking white babies?*

Bruce and Foxx not only influenced but also eased the path for Richard Pryor, one of the twentieth century's comic geniuses. After achieving some success as a "white-bread" comedian who admittedly mimicked Bill Cosby, Pryor dropped out of show business in the late sixties. When he returned, he had abandoned his nice-guy image and adopted a stage persona that still largely defines comics with attitude.

Like Lenny Bruce, Pryor drew heavily on society's peripheral people (winos, pimps, prostitutes, and hustlers) for his humor. But he also used experiences common to most African-Americans. Commenting on a court appearance, he quipped, "They give niggers time like it's lunch down there. You go down there lookin' for justice, that's what you find, just us!" And, in a bit about conflicting black and white perceptions of policemen, he offered: "White folks get a ticket they pull over. . . . 'Hey, officer, yes, glad to be of help . . . cheerio!' Niggers got to be talkin' 'bout, 'I am reaching into my pocket for my license, 'cause I don't want to be no motherfuckin' accident.'"

Cocky, candid, and sometimes crass, Pryor deftly revealed the full satiric range of a brash, assertive attitude in stand-up comedy. And, as his frequent television appearances (including his own NBC specials in 1977) demonstrated, he could be both funny and trenchant even when he avoided obscene language. Nearly all of the truly assertive comedians who followed Pryor cite his blunt, forthright approach as the inspiration for their own humor.

Eddie Murphy was the first to emerge as a star during the eighties and nineties. In such routines as the Velvet Jones "How to Be a Ho" bit he unveiled

Lenny Bruce

I get women, too. I can't keep 'em, but I get 'em. Women always leave me, man. I don't mind them leaving, but they tell you why. Know what I mean? Just leave, don't tell me why! . . . Drive you to drink, Jack. I tried drinking for a while but I used to go into bars and check out the people that were drinking, and they weren't happy. And they get beat up a lot.

Richard Pryor
Saturday Night Live, 1975

I'll tell you something else, about this Doors movie and this whole sixties revival, do we need a two-hour movie about Jim Morrison and the Doors? No we don't. I'll sum it up for you in five seconds. "I'm drunk— I'm nobody; I'm drunk—I'm famous; I'm drunk—I'm dead." Okay? There's the whole movie for you right there. I'm not wearing bell-bottoms again, I don't care what happens with the Doors movie, I don't care what comes out of Manchester, I'm not wearing the bell-bottoms again, okay? I wore 'em once and I didn't get laid, alright?

Denis Leary
London Underground, 1992

Denis Leary

Anybody got cable? I been watching a lot of cable lately 'cos I'm so mad at—the only good show on TV now is Star Trek. *That's some good shit. I like Captain Kirk and shit, Captain Kirk will fuck anybody. I seen him beam down on a planet. . . ever see the episode he fucked this green bitch? You gotta be a horny motherfucker to fuck a green bitch. I mean I ain't no racist, but if the bitch is green there's something wrong with the pussy.*

Eddie Murphy
Delirious, 1983

during his stint as a *Saturday Night Live* regular, he revealed a brazen satirical bent: "Are you a female high-school dropout between the ages of sixteen and twenty-five? Are you tired o' lying around in bed all day with nothin' to do? Well, you need never get up again, because in six short weeks I can train you to be a high-payin' ho." And, in his HBO special *Delirious* and later concert film, *Raw*, he not only confirmed his mastery of comic mimicry with impressions of such celebrities as Bill Cosby, Elvis Presley, and Stevie Wonder, but also began shading his tough-guy approach with a brash brand of hip-hop machismo.

The comics-with-attitude venue found more hysterical and vindictive exponents in the late Sam Kinison and Andrew Dice Clay. Kinison could be almost rabid as he shrieked and ranted his way through a routine in which he ridiculed everything from gays and women to minorities, and even such disaster victims as starving Ethiopians: "This is sand," he suggested telling the latter. "Nothing grows here! Know what it's gonna be like in a hundred years? It's gonna be sand. You live in a fucking desert! We have deserts in America—we just don't live in them! Why don't you move to where the food is?"

Clay, who affected the part of a leather-jacketed Italian stud in his stand-up act, berated similar targets with as much or more rancor. Onstage, his favorite epithets for women were "bitch" and "slut." And, when not boasting of his prodigious sexual exploits, he would either dally with suggestive doggerel or drift into splenetic mockery of panhandlers, gays, Moonies, blacks, Hispanics, and immigrants of all persuasions. Clay's bon mots included such lines as, "A spic is a nigger with straight hair" and "They ought to have a sign at the airport saying, 'If you don't know the language, get the fuck outta the country.'"

Although as impious and profane as Clay or Kinison, Denis Leary has generally avoided crass sexist, homophobic, anti-immigrant, and anti-minority rantings. The fast-talking, irreverent, Irish Catholic tough-guy stage image that he established in the one-man show, *No Cure for Cancer*, veers more toward the so-called "sick" humor of the seventies than toward the studied nastiness of many contemporary comedians. As he says of himself, "Things that are bleak, you know, make me laugh."

Nowhere is that clearer than in his routine about Elvis and Jesus: "I'm glad Jesus died when he did. If Jesus had lived to be forty years old he would have ended up like Elvis. Come on, he had that big entourage of twelve guys willing to do anything he wanted. . . . He'd be walking around Jerusalem with a big fat beer belly and his black sideburns going,

> *Damn, I'm the son of God! Get me a cheeseburger and french fries right now.*
> *'But, Lord, you're overweight.'*
> *Shut up, or I'll turn you into a leper!*

I'm gonna go to hell for that, but I don't care."

Martin Lawrence, the star of Fox network's *Martin* and a frequent host of *Def Comedy Jam*, is probably the best known of the current crop of comics with attitude. Lawrence, as was Redd Foxx, is better known for his TV sitcom (in which he is torn between impressing his macho friends and sustaining a relationship with a strong black woman) than he is for his stand-up act. In the latter, he nearly always affects the in-your-face, crotch-grabbing bravado of the hood and leans toward physical comedy and bawdy routines that explore precoital hygiene and the intricacies of oral sex. He is, as producer Stan Lathan claims, "like a mirror of the current hip-hop generation."

At the opposite end of the spectrum from Lawrence's ribaldry is Paul Mooney's more cerebral confrontational comedy. His primary target is white

Sam Kinison

You wanna stop world hunger? Stop sending them food—don't send these people another bite, folks. You wanna send them something? You wanna help? Send them U-Hauls. Send them U-Hauls, some luggage, send them a guy out there that says, "Hey, you know, we've been driving out here every day with your food for, like, the last 134 years, and we've been driving out across the desert and it occurred to us there wouldn't be world hunger if you people would live where the food is! You live in a desert! You live in a fucking desert! Nothing grows out here! Nothing's gonna grow out here! You see this? This is sand! Yeah, it's sand! You know what it's gonna be 100 years from now? It's gonna be sand! You live in a fuckin' desert!"

Sam Kinison
The Ninth Annual Young Comedians
Special, *1985*

And, like, just as I was going out the door I passed this big dude walking round in circles with a picket sign, talkin' 'bout "Stop Abortion." So I said, "Motherfucker, when was the last time you was pregnant?"

And he looks at me, he says, "I don't have to discuss that with you."

I said, "Oh, but you should, because I have the answer to abortion."

He said, "What is it?"

I said, "Shoot your dick."

Whoopi Goldberg (as Fontaine, the junkie)
Direct from Broadway . . . , 1985

racism, and his tough attitude is apparent at the outset of his act: "White folks have no sense of humor about themselves. You can talk about everybody else and they'll sit and laugh all night. But talk about them and they'll get out of here. . . . Fuck you, you can be talked about too . . . this is America. Take it, you'll get over it. I got over it." Often, white audience members confirm Mooney's observation and walk out. Those who stay are treated to some pointedly funny social commentary. "White folks' favorite TV commercial is those little nigger raisins. They think it's cute. . . . I bet if I get me some marshmallows . . . and let 'em sing 'Surfing U.S.A.' they won't think that shit is so goddamn cute."

Comics with attitude, as we can see, come in many forms. They vary from folksy grandmother types and cerebral satirists to blonde bombshells, self-centered studs, and the frenetic demagogues whose work some critics have labeled "killer comedy" or "Sado Stand-up." This is no surprise, as another critic observed: "Comedy is both hatred and revel, rebellion and defense, attack and escape." Still, the best of these tough-minded comedians have tempered their verbal onslaughts with some introspection and self-criticism; the worst have given in to mean-spirited homophobia, sexism, and racism. What they have in common, however, is a willingness to push comedy toward the edge and broach taboo subjects that might otherwise remain unexplored. And, whether we are delighted, offended, or merely titillated, it is often their brash, irrepressible attitudes that command our attention.

Martin Lawrence hosting *Def Comedy Jam* (debuted in 1992)

WISEGUYS

"Yeah, Right": The Wiseguys

by Steve O'Donnell

Along with peanut butter and the revolver, America has given the world the Wiseguy—the sardonic, uppity Common Man. The "wise" part of his name is a joke and also a tribute, because while he's no Socrates, the Wiseguy really does make with the smart remarks. And all the synonyms—*wisenheimer, wiseacre, wiseass*— carry the same paradoxical connotation. He's trouble, he's annoying, but at the same time he's entertaining and brave. We urge the people we know not to be Wiseguys, but we love it when they do it well. And we all like to think that sometimes we're Wiseguys ourselves. It flatters us to think that the Wiseguy represents our national character, something like the cowboy. Well, Book-Reading-Broadcast-Comedy Aficionado, I'm here to tell you that the Wiseguy really does just that.

I'm not exactly dropping a sociopolitical bombshell here to point out that democracies produce the best Wiseguys. Fewer dungeons and firing squads and all. Plus, America's vaunted coarseness adds a special flavor to the vituperations of her untrammeled individuals. In a nutshell, we're *good* at not showing the proper respect for things.

It's the Wiseguy who says what ought to be said to embarrass authority and deflate pretension under the cover of the sarcastic comment and the casual come-back. He's the satirist in street clothes, who tosses off artful barbs at boobs and Babbits without leaving the coffee-and-doughnut ranks of Regular Joes. Yeah, he can be a little nasty, but under his cynical surface there's a slightly uncomfortable idealist. Not a preachy ideologue but a practical schmo, whose sense of humor is his best defense against the bullies and bullshit of the world. Life's thugs grab him by the lapels and he says "*You're wrinkling the material.*" To every glittering announcement by the White House or Madison Avenue, the Wiseguy rolls his eyes and offers what might be his signature phrase: "Yeah. Right."

A lot of Americans like to think they have this quality. And, God bless 'em, a lot of them do. It's a widely practiced amateur comedy style. But only a few individuals emerge in each generation who are focused and talented enough to do it professionally. In that way, our Wiseguy comedians can be admired and envied, like our purse-winning pro-bowlers and bass-fishing champions. They're like us—only more so.

Who are we talking about here? Well, Wiseguy aces range in personality type from the young Bob Hope of the thirties to the up-and-coming Bill Maher of the

Late Night with David Letterman
(1982–93)

Bob Hope

George Jessel

When an award-winning, prestigious doc-umentary crew goes to the trouble of rent-ing lights and cameras and catering trucks, and then goes out and hires a nonunion crew to shoot a documentary on America's comic voice, who do they choose? Not Hope, not Carson, not Gallagher—they chose me, okay? Me. M-e. Need I say more? All right. Not Joan Rivers, not David Bren-ner, not Woody Allen, they chose me, okay? Me—M fucking E. Need I say more? All right. Not Robin Williams, not Steve Mar-tin, not Richard Pryor, they chose me, okay, figure it out, they chose me. Now I know a lot of people are waiting in the wings—they wanna see me fail, they wanna see me bomb, they wanna see me play toilets for the rest of my career. But I know who you are, each and every one of you, and you're filth.

Richard Belzer
The Richard Belzer Show: "I, Belz," *1984*

The Marine Corps brass has voted pin-up pictures off-limits. They're gonna have those fellas over there cutting paper dolls. Next thing you know, they'll want 'em to stop smiling in their sleep.

Bob Hope
Chrysler Presents The Bob Hope Show: Shoot-In at NBC, *1967*

Richard Belzer

RICHARD BELZER

I have a house in France because of television. I was almost murdered by a crazed wrestler on live television before an audience of incredulous Americans. If you don't know what I'm talking about it's the famous Hulk Hogan–Richard Belzer incident on Hot Properties *[Belzer's talk show]. Because it was live and because it was on televi-sion in living color some people thought my blood was fake, but it was real. (Some people have show business in their blood, I had it on my jacket.) To make a long story short, I sued Hulk Hogan for his assault upon me. He settled out of court and now I have a house in France! Get it? . . . All thanks to the miracle of television.*

JACK CARTER

Without a doubt Milton Berle, the undisputed king, that maelstrom of mirth, was the biggest influence in my comedy life. As a kid, just to watch him at the Paramount Theater in New York firing off those rapid one-liners, quick asides, topical shtick was great.

One Saturday night, my NBC TV show, preceding Caesar and Coca, was on live from New York. My guest star was Buster Keaton, the great stone-faced clown. We were doing a routine about the billboard painters. After searching around on huge brushes attached to our feet like ice skates, we climbed ladders lying against a huge billboard mounted onstage. The billboard was supposed to fall gently with our weight and air pocket softly to the stage floor, but the billboard got caught in the overhead lights. There we hung, suspended precariously in midair for what seemed an eternity. Finally the billboard dropped without us as we hung onto the lights like two Harold Lloyds. All the while the audience was shrieking, and my mom in her usual front row seat, was yelling, "Come down Jack, it's not funny!" Buster Keaton looked over at me and from midair yelled, "This is a funnier finish than I had!" What a trouper!

Jack Carter

nineties, from absurdist practitioners like Groucho Marx to reality-obsessed monologuists like Dennis Miller. The flip Princes of Wiseguydom would include George Jessel and Richard Belzer, Garry Shandling and Jon Stewart, Will Rogers and David Letterman. All talented at the presentation of jokes, of course, but more importantly, all able *reactors*, because spontaneous response is what makes the Wiseguy a Wiseguy.

The first intense Wiseguy most of us encounter is in elementary school. He's rarely the jerk who's memorized a couple jokes from the Bazooka Joe wrappers. More often, he's a reckless guerrilla whose out-of-line answering-back classically lands him in the principal's office. These antics are described as bids for attention by psychologists, as if that were an unnatural impulse. "Don't get wise with me, young man," their teacher might threaten, unaware of the implicit contradiction to the stated aims of education.

May I risk waiting until this paragraph to assert what ought to be obvious to any non-idiot? Wiseguys are women too, and they make damn good Wiseguys, because so many have nurtured humorous skepticism as a survival tool right along. Brett Butler, Elayne Boosler, Roseanne, and Joan Rivers are top-of-the-line Wiseguys, bristling with all the verve and creative aggression of their male peers. (We could coin a term here incorporating the word "gals," but that, I'm pretty sure, would be a mistake.)

Our smart-alecky American heritage offers up Proto-Wiseguys like Mark

Woman at McDonald's drive-through: Can I have two cheeseburgers and a small order of fries?

Letterman, working behind the counter: You know, ma'am, we're really busy, can I ask you to circle the lot one time? Can you just go around like once or twice till we kind of collect ourselves here? If you don't mind it would really help us out a lot; we're just up to our necks here.

Woman: Who is this?

Letterman: None of your business. Just circle the lot and we'll pick you up the next time, all right?

David Letterman
Late Show with David Letterman, *1993*

Elayne Boosler

PHYLLIS DILLER

When I was a child I listened only to FUNNY radio. Bob Hope was my favorite and he always had interesting guests. I have adopted his one-liner style of delivery. I feel he is the most brilliant comic who ever lived.

The funniest thing that happened to me on nationwide television was when Tony Orlando grabbed me during my introduction on his show, bent me over backwards in that wonderful old-fashioned kissing position, and my wig fell off. He didn't know it till he brought me back up—with a wail of horror. It was one of the funniest moments of my life.

Twain and Ambrose Bierce. You could probably even include Benjamin Franklin, with his blithe toss-offs about all hanging together or all hanging separately. And today's Wiseguys have spiritual ancestors in the frontiersman and the private eye—independent operators with their own personal codes of honor. (I feel compelled to include such points because, you know, this being a real book published by a museum and all.) The American Wiseguy's family tree even includes a couple of nonhumans. (Bugs Bunny, for my money, represents Brooklyn-flavored Wiseguyery at its finest.)

It's tricky to generalize (thank God I'm not writing a guide to edible mushrooms), but the Wiseguy World includes some highly diverse types. At the outer edges might be artist-hipsters like Lenny Bruce and urbane raconteurs like Jack Paar. Not Common Man types exactly, but restless, verbally skilled commentators with an intolerance for the hypocrisy of modern society (a Big Bugaboo in our postwar era). At its functioning, meat-and-potatoes, stand-up comic center, Planet Wiseguy includes rambunctious zinger-mongers like Phil Silvers and Rodney Dangerfield. Don Rickles and Marsha Warfield. And, incidentally, wouldn't it be wonderful if somewhere there was a planet with meat-and-potatoes at its center?

How are these Wiseguy comedians different from the other varieties our fertile, show-biz drenched republic produces in such abundance? Well, the Wiseguy is a clown insofar as he likes to get a laugh, but his modus operandi rarely includes crossed eyes or seltzer down the pants. Likewise, elaborate Uncle Milty-style Cleopatra costumes are not for him. For Wiseguys, *attitude* is more important than props and pratfalls. And, as that teacher warned our comedian-in-embryo, *attitude* for Wiseguys means *bad attitude*. Will Rogers's comment about never meeting a man he didn't like notwithstanding, Wiseguys are not usually boosters. But it's possible to be negative in the service of a good cause, pointing out that the

Eddie: The last time you gave me a check it came back marked insufficient funds.

George: Insufficient funds! Two hundred dollars insuffic . . . What bank was it?

Eddie: The First National.

George: That's crazy. A big bank like that, and they haven't got two hundred dollars?

Eddie: They've got it. You haven't got it. You got nothing!

George: All right. . . Then get the money from them.

Eddie: But they don't owe me the money!

George: You don't know what you're doing.

Eddie: What do you mean?

George: You're lending money to the wrong people, see?

George Jessel and Eddie Cantor
Lincoln Mercury Startime: George Burns in "The Big Time," *1957*

[Cher's] got a commercial, she goes: "I call my perfume uninhibited 'cause there are so many different people in me." Yeah, and they're all under eighteen.

Joy Behar
The Best of Stand-Up Spotlight, *1993*

Phil Silvers as Sergeant Bilko (center) with Harvey Lembeck and Allan Melvin

Emperor has no clothes and all that. Let's call it *optimistic pessimism*—and thanks for playing along.

The Wiseguy comics don't usually come off as entertainers in the variety show sense of the word. Somehow, their just-stepped-out-of-the-crowd credibility would be tarnished by too much dancing. Yes, Bob Hope started out as a hoofer in vaudeville, and Dave Letterman is a fair juggler, drummer, and Jimmy Stewart impersonator, but these talents are secondary to their principal ability: making smart remarks about what's going on around them.

Let's add that they aren't really actors either, and if you see them in a movie or TV show they can't be much different than themselves. Some fine Wiseguy

"Mr. Television" Milton Berle with Phil Silvers

On Location special *Don Rickles and His Wise Guys* (1980)

DON RICKLES

I believe it was in 1978 that I was starring in an NBC series titled C. P. O. Sharkey, *which we did directly across the hall from* The Tonight Show. *At that time, I also used to guest host* The Tonight Show *frequently when Johnny Carson was on vacation. On one such occasion, while sitting at his desk, I accidentally broke Johnny's cigarette box. I laughed about it and made a joke. The next night, Johnny returned from vacation, and I was taping an episode of* Sharkey. *Upon discovering the broken cigarette box, Johnny, during* The Tonight Show, *brought his cameras across the hall and interrupted my taping as a surprise. He said something to the effect of, "If you think it's funny that you broke my cigarette box, you'll really find it funny if I ruin your show." Obviously, he was kidding the whole time, with his closing line being that he couldn't understand why* C. P. O. Sharkey *was even on the air and that I owed him a new cigarette box.*

Groucho Marx hosts *You Bet Your Life* (1950–61)

achievements in this area include Richard Belzer's role on *Homicide*, Don Rickles's work with Martin Scorsese, and Roseanne's solid ABC series. (Tip: rent *Cabin Boy*—and thank me later!)

Intangible as it is, Wiseguy-status can come and go, even for individual comics. Chevy Chase was briefly the nation's foremost Wiseguy, but his endorsement by Gerald Ford took some of the fun out of his parodies, and the comfort of Hollywood dulled the edge of what seemed at one time antiestablishment. The same problem can be seen with Will Rogers and Bob Hope, who eventually did a lot of socializing with the presidents and senators they joked about. A good Wiseguy rule-of-thumb: don't golf with The Material.

Really satisfying Wiseguys show some aggression and belligerence in their style. Before his song-and-dance days, Bob Hope was a boxer back in Cleveland, fighting under the name Packy East, and that had to help his sense of Wiseguy timing. We look forward to a degree of snideness in Dennis Miller's stand-up, and to some meanness in the teasing of Don Rickles. But a top-notch Wiseguy isn't just a hostile crank; he's got a sense of irony, and, not to get all high-falutin' about it, of justice. The phrase "cut 'em down to size" sums up the folk function of the Wiseguy.

If I may restate my theme: the Wiseguy represents the American character better than any other comic style. These funny men and women have a special democratic vitality, like banjos and Hershey Bars. I think we turn 'em out better here than anywhere else on earth. (If you feel differently, please keep it to yourself.)

They're heroes, aren't they?

Yeah. *Right.*

Don Rickles, after kissing a woman's hand: "What'd you have for dinner, fish?"

My wife takes off her bra at night and her head hits the sink.

Don Rickles
Rickles, 1975

. . . And now, a few unkind words about Ed Sullivan. Ed, everybody's been up here kidding you about your personality. I can't understand it—after all, it's pretty hard to talk about something that isn't there. Personally, I've seen more personality in a hot water bottle. . . . But I will say this Ed, with all insincerity. I've known you a long time, that's true, and I've been on your show twenty times—maybe someday you're going to cough up a little money and surprise everybody. But you will, you will be on television a long time because the amount of talent you have will certainly never wear out, I'll tell you that right now.

Jack E. Leonard
The Friars Club Man of the Hour:
Ed Sullivan, *1956*

About the Contributors

ANNE BEATTS, a television writer-producer, won two Emmys as a writer for the original *Saturday Night Live*. She created and produced the critically acclaimed CBS sitcom *Square Pegs*, and was coexecutive producer for the first year of NBC's long-running hit series *A Different World*. Her many other television projects include sketches for *Comic Relief* and *The Little Mermaid* for *Faerie Tale Theatre*. With her partner, John Kalish, she is executive producer of the nationally syndicated late-night comedy talk show starring Stephanie Miller. The first woman contributing editor of the *National Lampoon*, she is a regular contributor to *Mirabella* and *Elle*.

DAVID BUSHMAN has been curator of television and advertising at The Museum of Television & Radio since 1992. Previously he was senior editor of television at *Variety* in New York before assuming that same title at *Daily Variety* in Los Angeles. He has also worked for *Billboard* and numerous newspapers.

DOUGLAS COUPLAND, a contributing editor to *Wired* magazine, is the author of *Generation X, Shampoo Planet, Life After God,* and *Microserfs.*

LARRY GELBART has written for radio, television, the stage, and screen. He received Emmy Awards for the television series *M*A*S*H* (which he developed for television) and *Barbarians at the Gate;* Tony Awards for coauthoring *A Funny Thing Happened on the Way to the Forum* and for his book of the musical *City of Angels;* Oscar nominations for his screenplays for *Oh, God* and *Tootsie,* as well as an Outer Critics Circle Award for his contributions to comedy.

TONY HENDRA was editor of the *National Lampoon* from 1971 through 1978. His political and social satire also includes the 1995 film *The Great White Hype;* the British television series *Spitting Image,* which he cocreated, produced, and wrote; *Lemmings,* the 1973 review he directed; and his por-

trayal of band manager "Ian Faith" in rock's cult classic *This Is Spinal Tap.* Among the bestselling books Mr. Hendra has edited or cowritten are *Not the New York Times, The 80s: A Look Back, Going Too Far,* and *The Book of Bad Virtues.*

MERLE KESSLER is the author of *I Gotta Go, Ian Shoales' Perfect World,* and coauthor (with Dan Coffey) of *The 'Ask Dr. Science' Big Book of Science,* and *Dr. Science's Book of Shocking Domestic Revelations.* Playwright, actor, and founding member of Duck's Breath Mystery Theatre, he is currently employed by Sega of America as a writer of interactive games.

MARVIN KITMAN is the television critic for *Newsday* and his syndicated column appears in papers nationally. He is author of *I Am a VCR,* a chronicle of his twenty-plus years as a critic; *The Marvin Kitman Show: Encyclopedia Televisiana;* and *George Washington's Expense Account,* among other books. On television, he has done commentary for New York stations WPIX and WNEW, and cocreated the sitcom *Ball Four* for CBS.

DENIS LEARY is perhaps best known for his one-man show *No Cure for Cancer,* which won the Critics Award in 1990 when it premiered at the Edinburgh International Arts Festival before successful runs in London and New York. As a film actor he has appeared in *The Ref, Judgment Night,* and *The Sandlot,* among others. As a director, Mr. Leary has done short pieces for cable television's Showtime. He is a contributing editor to *Details,* and has also written for *Playboy* and *New York* magazines.

PATRICIA MARX was the first woman to write for the *Harvard Lampoon,* and has since published in the *New Yorker, Atlantic,* the *New York Times,* and *Spy.* She was a staff writer for *Saturday Night Live* and has written for the children's programs *Clarissa Explains It All* and *Rugrats* for Nickelodeon and *Little Lulu* for HBO. Ms. Marx has written several screenplays; along with Douglas McGrath, she wrote the play *Dominoes* and the satiric novel *Blockbuster*. Ms. Marx has also written the children's book *Now Everybody Really Hates Me*.

ELVIS MITCHELL, entertainment critic for NPR's *Weekend Edition with Scott Simon*, is also editor at large for *Spin* magazine. A former contributing editor at *Rolling Stone* and *Interview*, he survived the late night panel show *Last Call*. He has written for *GQ, Vogue*, the *New York Times Magazine*, and the *London Observer* and contributed pieces to the BBC/PBS coproduction *Edge*, a magazine show.

STEVE O'DONNELL has written for David Letterman since 1982. He served as head writer on the NBC *Late Night* program for nine years. His freelance work has appeared in *Rolling Stone, Playboy, Spy*, and the *New York Times*.

GEORGE PLIMPTON is founder and editor of the *Paris Review*. As a participatory journalist he has played for the Detroit Lions, the Boston Celtics, and the New York Philharmonic, and has explored many other professional worlds including the circus, photography, bullfighting, fireworks, and stand-up comedy. His many books include *Out of My League, Paper Lion, Edie: An American Biography,* and *The X-Factor*. Mr. Plimpton has served as an associate editor at *Harper's* and *Horizon* magazines and is a special contributor to *Sports Illustrated*.

HOWARD ROSENBERG is television critic for the *Los Angeles Times;* his column reaches hundreds of papers nationwide via the *Washington Post/Los Angeles Times* wire. He has won the Pulitzer Prize and the Edward R. Murrow Award for his criticism. Mr. Rosenberg has also written for *Rolling Stone* and *Spin* magazines and is an adjunct professor at University of Southern California and California State University, Northridge. He was named a recipient of the 1995 USC Journalism Alumni Association Award.

MEL WATKINS is the author of *On The Real Side*, a history of African-American humor from slavery to Richard Pryor. He is a contributor to the *New York Times Book Review*, where he has also served as an editor, and the Arts & Leisure section of the *Times*. His writing has appeared in the *New York Times Magazine, New York* magazine, *Entertainment Weekly*, the *Southern Review*, and *Black Review*. Mr. Watkins's memoir of his childhood, *Dancing With Strangers*, will be published in 1996.

Acknowledgments

The Museum of Television & Radio gratefully acknowledges all of the individuals and companies that donated programming used in the preparation of this book and for the exhibition, including:

Brillstein-Grey Entertainment; Broadway Video; Capital Cities/ABC, Inc.; Carsey-Werner; Susan Rubio and Jeff Sotzing of Carson Productions; CBS Inc.; Columbia Tri-Star Television; Comedy Central; Bibbi Herrmann of Comic Relief; John Davies of John Davies Productions; Ira Gallen; Lee Salas of Group W Video; Bob Henry; Home Box Office; Knave Productions, Inc.; the Library of Congress; Meadowlane Enterprises Inc.; NBC Entertainment; Paramount; Research Video; George Schlatter; George Shapiro of West/Shapiro & Associates; Michele Armour and Chuck Sutton of *It's Showtime at the Apollo!;* Showtime Networks; Andrew Susskind; 20th Television; Dan Einstein, UCLA Film and Television Archive; Warner Bros. Television; Robert B. Weide; and William Korn of Westinghouse Broadcasting Company, Inc.

We also thank Scott Carter, Mel Watkins, and Tim Williams for sharing their expertise on comedy.

As our publisher, we could not have asked for a more committed house than Harry N. Abrams. We would like to thank Paul Gottlieb for his support of this project from the beginning, Robert Morton, our helpful and insightful editor, and the book's designer Ellen Nygaard Ford.

In the world of publishing and rights, the timely responses from Richard Sugarman of The Hearst Corporation and Anne Sibbald of Janklow & Nesbit Associates to our endless queries were tremendously valuable. Also a thank you to our friend Danny Grover of CAA for his generous guidance and advice on this project.

We would especially like to thank General Motors, our partner in presenting the *Stand-Up Comedians on Television* exhibition. General Motors's support of this project demonstrates its continued commitment to quality television.

For help with photo research, we would like to acknowledge Ray Whelan, Jr., at Globe Photos and Howard and Ron Mandelbaum at Photofest.

An exhibition and publication of this magnitude required the efforts and talents of the entire Museum staff. The following people in particular were integral to the completion of this book and the exhibition:

In the Curatorial Department: Susan Fisher, Vice President; Ron Simon, Curator, Television; Ken Mueller, Manager, Radio Department; Alden Gewirtz and Judith Dieckmann, Researchers; Abbey Benowitz, Myles Reiff, and Gary Rutkowski, Curatorial Assistants; in the Publications Department: Donna Levy, Editorial

Assistant; in Technical Services: Tom Fleming, Videotape Editor, and Ann Marie Aversano, Andrea Begor, Jake Diamond, James Kreyling, and Tracy Martin, Tape Transfer Technicians; in the Registrar's Office: Hunter Brown, Registrar; in Research Services: Jonathan Rosenthal, Researcher; in the Education Department: Dale Zaklad, Director, and Ritty Burchfield, Coordinator, Satellite Seminars; in Public Relations: Todd Merrill, Director, and Gina Jarrin Keir, Senior Publicist; in Development: Susan Davis, Manager, Corporate and Foundation Relations; for business affairs: Patrick S. Gallagher, Vice President; and in Public Affairs and Programs: Elizabeth Meyer, Assistant, and Diane Lewis, Vice President, who helps to keep it all moving with good humor.

Special Thanks

Above all, this publication and exhibition would not have been possible without the talents and dedication of Jennifer Lewis, Assistant Curator; Allen Glover, Researcher; and Ari Vena, Assistant to the Vice President of Curatorial Services, who spent countless hours viewing programs and helped to conceptualize the screening series.

Index

Note: Italic numbers refer to illustrations.